I Am Different from You

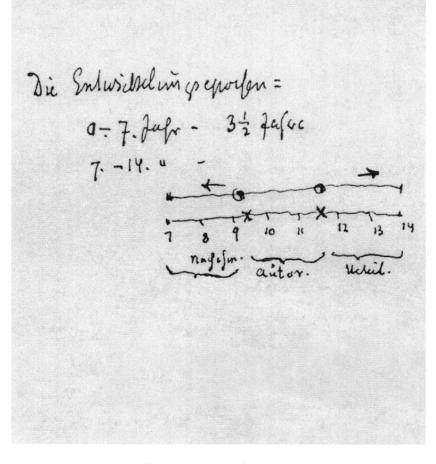

The Developmental stages =

Imitation   Authority   Judgment

From the middle third of a notebook entry by Rudolf Steiner
in *Die Waldorfschule und ihr Geist*, GA 297, p. 293.

I Am Different from You

from You

How Children Experience Themselves and

the World in the Middle of Childhood

Peter Selg

2011

SteinerBooks

SteinerBooks
610 Main Street, Great Barrington, MA 01230
www.steinerbooks.org

Translated by Margot M. Saar.

Originally published in German by Verlag des Ita Wegman Instituts 2011 as *Ich bin anders als du. Vom Selbst- und Welterleben des Kindes in der Mitte der Kindheit.*

Library of Congress Cataloging-in-Publication Data

Selg, Peter, 1963-
[Ich bin anders als du. English]
I am different from you : how children experience themselves and the world in the middle of childhood / Peter Selg.
    p. cm.
"Originally published in German by Verlag des Ita Wegman Instituts 2011 as Ich bin anders als du. Vom Selbst- und Welterleben des Kindes in der Mitte der Kindheit"– T.p. verso.
Includes bibliographical references.
ISBN 978-0-88010-658-0
1. Waldorf method of education. 2. Steiner, Rudolf, 1861-1925. 3. Self-perception in children. I. Title.
LB1029.W34S4613 2011
371.39'1 – dc22
                                        2011035848

Printed in the United States

Contents

Me, I'm myself,
no one in this big
world is like me.
I am different from you
and everyone else.
I'm just plain old
Me.
Me, I'm myself,
no one's like me,
and I'm not like anyone,
I'm just myself
Little old me.
I'm not quite sure what
makes me different,
I suppose it's in my ways.
No one's the same
especially me.

Pat Kirk[1]

Introduction

IN MANY OF HIS LECTURES ON EDUCATION Rudolf Steiner called attention to a significant change in the way children experience themselves and the world. This change, which is often overlooked, occurs in the "middle of childhood," when the children are in their ninth or tenth year. Steiner spoke of a "dramatic change in the child's consciousness,"[2] a crisis that, unlike the crises of adolescence, is hardly noticeable to the observer. "There comes a time when children show, not in what they say but in their whole behavior, that they are struggling with a question or a number of questions that are indicative of a crisis in their soul life. It is a very subtle experience for the child, which requires an equally subtle response. But it is there, and it does need attention."[3]

Rudolf Steiner spoke about this crisis, especially to the Waldorf teachers, because it was important to him to make those in charge of educating children aware of this phenomenon. It was Steiner's hope that teachers would in the future devote more attention to the individual child, and he offered them the necessary tools to do so. He also hoped that less overt developmental steps, such as the "subtle" inner crisis of the ninth or tenth year, would one day be given the kind of attention they require and that is their due. Children experience an inner instability of which teachers and educators are in fact an integral part.[4] Teachers are therefore called upon to support the children in their individual developmental crises, even if the "crisis symptoms" are very contained. If there is no outer traumatization, children in their ninth or tenth year will pass through the developmental stage that belongs to that age without displaying alarming signs of distress. But it is all the more important, as Steiner pointed out, that we attend with loving attention and care to this (physiologically and psychologically) crucial stage and to the children who rely on us as adults during that time: "Children do not usually express what really troubles them, but something else. We must be aware of the fact that what they express comes from the depths of their soul. And we need to know what to say and how to behave because our response will be crucial for the child's entire future life."[5]

Rudolf Steiner's detailed descriptions of this challenging developmental event refer to the relationship that children have with their own self and with the world. In the ninth or tenth year, the relationship changes or is newly configured, and in that process children experience the loss of the foundations that used to "naturally" support and carry them in life. In his anthroposophical approach to developmental physiology and psychology Rudolf Steiner did not play down the importance of the—generally widely discussed—disruptions and crises of self-discovery that come with puberty. He devoted much attention to the "grand metamorphosis" of adolescence, and his thoughts on the theme are still highly relevant today.[6] At the same time, Steiner made it quite clear that the various aberrations, failures, inabilities, and disorders (if not illnesses) of adolescence cannot be reduced just to the specific difficulties and challenges of youth. They largely trace back to the much more "subtle" events that occur in the middle of the second seven-year period. This means that what happens at the earlier age has tremendous prophylactic potential. The forces, (self-) awareness, social skills, and general mood of teenagers at the crucial stage of puberty and adolescence depend greatly on the inner experiences they had in the middle of childhood. Pediatric psychologists and psychiatrists know well that many fears and weaknesses that rise to the surface later, originate at that time.

The reductionist or positivist approach commonly applied in physiology and developmental psychology is unable to discover what really happens in the body, soul, and spirit of children in the middle of childhood.[7] What we need is a more profound understanding of the situation at this particular age if we want to find the right way of helping and supporting the child, and if we want to know "what to say and how to behave."[8] Rudolf Steiner's fundamental contributions to this field are not only milestones of a true anthropology, they offer viable pedagogical perspectives. As in all his pedagogical writings and lectures, he focused here on the situation of the child. Steiner did not propose that we leave the—considerable—developmental challenges of the middle of childhood to psychotherapists. He hoped that teachers and parents, once they had gained the necessary insights, would know what to do and when to do it. In order to be able to create the right conditions and pedagogical relationship for this crisis we need profound knowledge of the child's situation, that is, of the child's inner essence at this time: of the prevailing forces, concerns and questions.

Steiner never encouraged teachers or parents to overwhelm children with questions or force them to speak about their soul life—which is mostly semi-conscious, in any case. The right word, the right behavior toward the child would emerge, as he said, out of our heightened attention toward the child, out of an atmosphere that we cannot create through the spoken word— the main tool of a culture that relies primarily on cognition and verbalization—but through intense "selfless awareness" of the other person, of the child.[9] The crisis of the middle of childhood arises from the transformation of the relationship that nine- to ten-year-olds have to the world and to their own self. Our response to this crisis must arise, in the first instance, from the relationship we have established and fostered through our teaching. *"The relationship we establish to the child at that time is eminently important for the child's whole life."*[10] If we do not succeed in establishing this kind of relationship with the children, they will have to continue their journey through life without the experience of being carried by a strong attachment. Rudolf Steiner said about this in a lecture:

> When children cross the Rubicon between the ninth and tenth year without that feeling, something will be lacking in their later life, and they will have to struggle to attain what they should have received naturally at that moment in childhood.[11]

*

Seeing how much our civilization has changed, it is entirely legitimate to ask at the beginning of the twenty-first century whether Rudolf Steiner's developmental theory of almost one hundred years ago is still relevant. A number of recent publications deal with generational changes and the different ways in which children grow up and develop in today's high-tech world. Rudolf Steiner never specified a particular year or age for these crises. He knew about developmental acceleration. In a lecture on the symptoms of the crisis in the middle of childhood he said: "It can easily happen today that children present such symptoms quite early."[12] Rudolf Steiner was not concerned with dates and figures. It was important to him to make teachers aware of the situation so that they would recognize it and support the children through it in the right way. That aspect is unlikely to have changed much during the twentieth century. The forces at work in children, who are trying to find their own inner balance at that point in their development, have remained the same despite the change in outer conditions. It is an undoubted achievement of Rudolf Steiner's anthroposophical anthropology to have identified these forces. He was able to found his new approach to education, curative education, and medicine on his spiritual-scientific findings.

This book is an anthology of Rudolf Steiner's references to the events in the "middle of childhood." Hans Müller-Wiedemann,

an excellent physician and curative teacher, devoted a compre-
hensive scientific study to the same topic in 1973, in which he
discussed in great depth Rudolf Steiner's spiritual-scientific findings and their relevance to developmental psychology and physiology.[13] I owe Rudolf Steiner and Hans Müller-Wiedemann the
inspiration for my own, more modest work that is published by
the Ita Wegman Institute in a series of monographs on developmental physiology and pedagogy based on spiritual science.[14]
While Müller-Wiedemann's work was intended as a contribu-
tion to the scientific discourse on the various aspects of this
particular developmental crisis, the present book indicates ways
of responding to the crisis in question out of a deeper understanding of anthroposophical anthropology. For this endeavor
Rudolf Steiner's considerations and methods prove invaluable.
"We must learn to observe the child. We must feel our way into
the child [...]" (Rudolf Steiner).[15]

PETER SELG

Director of the Ita Wegman Institute
for Basic Research into Anthroposophy

1.

I Am Myself

Changes of the soul life

People nowadays are much more concerned with the outer than the inner life, and they give too little attention to the changes that take place in the ninth or tenth year.

Rudolf Steiner[16]

THE DRAMATIC CHANGES that mark the middle of childhood were often described by Rudolf Steiner as an abrupt occurrence, a distinct "point" or "moment" in life, when a conscious or semi-conscious world- and self-awareness awakens in the child: "*Suddenly* children see the world with different eyes. It is like an awakening, as if they were entering into a very special relationship with their own self." [17]

In various pedagogical contexts Rudolf Steiner explained that the "point in time" for these inner soul changes was usually after the ninth birthday. "Around the ninth year," [18] "around the time when the child turns nine," [19] "at the age of about nine and a half," [20] children reached a turning point. It could happen slightly sooner or later, occasionally even *before* the ninth year, [21] or between the age of nine and ten and a half, [22] if not eleven…. [23] "Around the ninth year, it could also be in the tenth or eleventh year…" [24] "*We have to be acutely aware [...] of the individuality that comes to expression in each child….*" [25] According to Rudolf Steiner all children experience this change even though it is not always overt, or might be prevented or hindered to an extent by cultural influences. [26]

"*There is a brief moment between the ages of nine and ten, closer to the ninth year, when children begin to see themselves increasingly as separate from their surroundings.*" [27] In their soul life as well as in their objective experience of the world, children begin to "separate their I from the surrounding world." [28] They learn to differentiate between their own self and the world of which they used to be an integral part:

> We need to be aware of the fact that before the age of nine or ten children are unable to differentiate between their own self and the world around them. They might, instinctively, have referred to themselves as "I" before, but they nevertheless felt they were an inherent part of the world. They experienced the whole world as akin to themselves. [...] Everything was one for them and they were part of this unity. Only when they turn nine or ten do they learn to see themselves as distinct from the world around them.[29]

Rudolf Steiner referred to this moment as a "becoming aware that I am an I and the world is outside me,"[30] an awakening experience similar to being astounded, both in the moment of first awareness and in the following weeks and months. "... children come to be truly astounded about all that goes on in the world, *because they begin to perceive themselves in the world* ...."[31] With this dramatic moment of separation children lose the naïve openness to the world, they no longer inhabit and experience the world in natural unawareness.

Children refer to themselves as "I" much earlier, at around the age of three when they take a significant developmental hurdle—"when at a deeper level, out of the language, emerges a sense of 'you are an I'."[32] Despite the seeming self-awareness of that gesture, it is the verbal manifestation of a step forward in the development of consciousness[33] that does not herald the true separation from the world. Children continue to be at one with parents, attachment figures, nature, and objects and feel a close affinity to the world around them. ("Although the children, somehow instinctively, speak of themselves as "I" [at that time], they feel that they are an inherent part of the world. They experience the whole world as akin to themselves."[34]) But then, around the ninth year, the "process of separation from the environment" sets in as "world experience and self experience become separate."[35] According to Rudolf Steiner this is an unexpected and brief event, an entirely new phenomenon that emerges at a particular moment and initiates a development that will go on for several years, reaching its intended completion in adolescence when it will manifest as inner independence.

*

This dramatic birth of consciousness affects children's relationship with the world and with their own self. It is not a reflective process but primarily one of *feeling*: "It is all in the feeling, but it is therefore the more intense and the more in need of attention."[36] Children are not able to articulate what is going on but they observe an "essential enhancement, or compression, of their *I-experience*.[37] This self-experience is intensified and deepened in the soul realm, in the feeling.[38] Steiner spoke of an actual transition from awareness to self-awareness in child development,[39] from the burgeoning first contact with their own I—in the sphere of feeling—to the manifestation of their true individuality. Children discover "a very special relationship with their own I"[40] and, out of this feeling, they begin to form a real I-concept.[41] In the third year, when the child first says "I," the I enters the human soul. Now, the I-awareness becomes "spiritual"[42] which means that the soul life emancipates itself increasingly.

The experiences that accompany this event can be intense and striking enough to be remembered in later life. The composer Bruno Walter wrote about himself as a child:

> [...] The growing boy was often in a strange "dreamy" state, absorbed or engrossed in nothing in particular, with all the wheels that were usually driven fast by the torrential stream of outer and inner impressions having come to a halt. —I still remember when that stillness occurred

for the first time within me like a melancholy sensation. I still feel what I felt then and can see the place in front of me where, as a boy *of about ten or eleven*, I had felt this inner shudder. I cannot remember how it came about that I stood in the school playground all by myself. I might have been returning from a period of detention. I stepped out onto the huge playground that I had always known as filled with the noise of playing and running children, and that therefore seemed to me doubly empty and deserted. I can see myself standing there, overwhelmed by the profound silence, and while listening to this silence and to the light breeze, I feel how, out of the loneliness, something unknown and powerful touches my heart. It was the first time it vaguely occurred to me that I was an I, the first time it dawned on me that I had a soul and that something was calling to this soul from somewhere.[43]

Walter described the dawning of I-awareness in the middle of childhood as occurring in "profound silence" and "loneliness," culminating in a first conscious or almost-conscious experience of his own existence with its particular inner and outer circumstances. Christy Brown was born in Ireland, the tenth of twenty-two children. He was severely disabled, and because of athetosis, could only control his left foot. He wrote in his autobiography, *My Left Foot,* how he grew conscious of his special circumstances only in his tenth year:

I was now just ten, a boy who couldn't walk, speak, feed, or dress himself. I was helpless, but only now did I begin to realize how helpless I really was. I still didn't know anything about myself: I knew nothing beyond the fact that I was "different" from others. [...] Up to then I had never thought about myself. [...] I had gone on playing with my brothers, enjoying the little bit of life that I saw, all the time unconscious of myself.[44]

*

Some children are able to express in words what they experience in the middle of childhood as they "feel their way into the language."[45] The awareness of one's being separate from the world, when it first emerges, is tied to language. Children develop "because they struggle with language."[46] Their relationship with language changes as they begin to attach a deeper, more inward meaning to words. Children now link feeling and memory, they become aware of the fact that the words originate inside them.[47] Hans Müller-Wiedemann collected remarkable testimonies and poems from children of that age (*I am a living poem / I write no words*[44]):

> Me, I'm myself,
> no one in this big
> world is like me.
> I am different from you
> and everyone else.
> I'm just plain old
> Me.
> Me, I'm myself,
> no one's like me,
> and I'm not like anyone,
> I'm just myself
> Little old me.
> I'm not quite sure what
> makes me different,
> I suppose it's in my ways.
> No one's the same
> especially me.[49]

Such written testimonies, cautiously communicated in private, lyrical messages, are unusual. Although there is no doubt that the events described by Rudolf Steiner surge up in the child's soul as "vague feelings,"[50] they will remain concealed and unexpressed in most cases. The changes in attitude and behavior that can be observed around the ninth year hardly ever find expression in what children are able or willing to articulate. It is usually something else that first becomes apparent. In a lecture to teachers Rudolf Steiner observed: "We notice a kind of outer restlessness in the children. They cannot cope with the world around them. They feel a need to become shy. They somehow withdraw from the world. In a subtle and intimate way this happens with almost every child."[51]

*

In the twenty-first century with its rapidly expanding communication technologies and excessive distractions, the subtle changes that are part of the middle of childhood often go unnoticed. Because the soul is never at rest, children, parents, and teachers are hardly aware of what is happening. Yet, the ongoing externalization and materialization in the way we live, the "realism" that seeks to diminish or eliminate the sensitivities of the soul, cannot prevent the dramatic change altogether. It will happen in one way or another. Often it comes with a sudden pausing or moment of *stillness*, as described by Bruno Walter ("with all the wheels that were usually driven fast by the torrential stream of outer and inner impressions, having come to a halt ...").

The tendency to withdraw, to which Rudolf Steiner called attention repeatedly in the first two decades of the twentieth century, is noticeable, as is the augmented (reactive) need for parental closeness and support (even "clinginess") of which he also spoke.[52] Children might feel lonely or deserted, they might develop fears (even anti-social behaviors) that will affect all further development. In many cases, the naturally carrying foundations of life suddenly collapse and are no longer available. If, with Jacob and Wilhelm Grimm, we define crisis as a decisive state *"where the old and the new are in conflict,"*[53] the middle of childhood is just such a crisis. For the first time, the life lived so far becomes part of the child's conscious or close-to-conscious memory. Rudolf Steiner described how, around the ninth year, a "special relationship develops between the life of feeling and that of memory."[54] Children begin to realize (in a pre-conscious, close-to-conscious, or initially conscious way) that they have their own biography, their own individual life-story. They feel they are leaving behind childhood as they knew it. A new relationship to time emerges, to their life-time, just as the relationship to space changed in the third year with the very first awakening of the I.[55] By experiencing time and the actuality of existence and sentience, and by becoming aware of what belongs to the past, what belongs to the life that has been experienced and (to an extent) completed, children develop a sense of biography.[56] The new consciousness of the *transience* of existence is part of this process. The psychiatrist and philosopher Karl Jaspers remembered his own self-experience in the middle of childhood:

> I was ten years old [...] when I first experienced the painful, almost total memory of the *unfathomable having-lived* when I read a poem by Rückert in a school book: "From my youth a song resounds forever; alas how far gone is now what was once mine." — It was like having lost something and becoming aware at the same time of the infinite wealth I had already received. The mood of distance, united with the feeling of sacredness of the unattainable that was still part of me, made my soul grow wider and threatened to break my heart at the same time.[57]

Jasper's "total memory of the unfathomable having-lived" refers to the child's own origin, the world of childhood as history that precedes the present. Around the ninth year many children question the authenticity of their parents for the first time and worry that they might be adopted. Half-consciously, their feeling soul looks back, often with melancholy overtones ("it was like having lost something"). The experience of what is now and what is (irrevocably) gone, that first sense of the temporality of one's own life-story as clearly distinguishable from the pure present, from the "here and now" of the young child, implies the experience of continuity *and* discontinuity. The first awareness of what is gone and lost includes the first conscious encounter with death and dying. Unlike adolescents, children in the middle of childhood do not willfully plan their future. Their experience of the finiteness of existence—also of their *own* existence—comes out of the meeting of the present with the past or with transience.

The philosopher Ernst Bloch gave a striking account of himself in the middle of childhood:

> It came over me on a bench in the woods, and *I experienced myself as the one experiencing himself*, as the one who looked out, of whom one would never be able to rid oneself, awful and wonderful at the same time, the one who will sit in his hut with a globe. The one whom one will always have in reserve, even when he is one among many, the one who will ultimately die alone.[58]

The painter Oskar Kokoschka remembered his first encounter with death during that developmental phase: when he heard that a storyteller who had lived very close to his parents' house had passed away:

> I could not quite understand what having died meant. I just realized that she had disappeared for good ... *I can never disappear, I thought.* Of course she is not here, but she must be somewhere.

Two days later the young Oskar saw the hearse with the white coffin:

For a long time I watched as the strange vehicle passed on. [...] I suddenly had the dull feeling that the outside world must have its limits. I experienced irretrievability, and it was like moving from the light of day to a predestined, frightening night.[59]

The following poem was not written by an adult reflecting on life, but by a child in the middle of childhood:

> The poor tree withers.
> It withers and dies.
> No one cares, they just
> walk by.
> Once it was a lovely
> tree, so high it almost
> reached the sky.
> Just like anything else
> it dies.
> Poor tree.[60]

*

With the newly-felt awareness of one's self and of one's separateness from the world, the relationship to the other person, to the "you," also changes. It is not until now that children realize the separateness of others. Rudolf Steiner often mentioned how children, up to the middle of childhood, feel deeply connected with their primary attachment figures and with other important people around them. Mother and father are not only part of the surrounding world, they are part of the child's body.[61] For the child, the relationship is based on trust and love. The child imitates and looks up to the adults without perceiving their inner life or autonomy. The ability to see others as personalities in their own right only begins in the middle of childhood. It arises from the children's new awareness of their own self and their own existence. As they develop a true sense of self, children become aware of the "you" for the first time. They no longer feel they are one with the other, but see others as autonomous beings who have an inner life of their own. "I am different from you / *and anybody else.*"

As part of this process the children's social relationships and playful interactions begin to change.[62] We observe how children enter into relationships that are increasingly informed by a sense of solidarity, loyalty, and friendship that is based on mutual recognition. Hans Müller-Wiedemann demonstrated this in a compelling way:[63] The friendships that the children seek and find ("Children now leave the realm of past, familiar habits and enter their *own* individual present"[64]) do not primarily arise from shared interests and are hardly acts of intelligence or socialization. They are amazing in that they are based on mutual acceptance without any expectations. If the friendships are not distorted due to inappropriate cultural influences, they arise from a waking up to the other's differentness, to the significance of friendship as such, from an atmosphere of equality and togetherness that enables the individuals involved to find themselves and not lose faith in themselves. "The deep mystery and stillness of these friendships rest on a reassuring sense of 'being together' which, in itself, confirms one's own existence" (Müller-Wiedemann).[65] The other, the You, the friend, becomes the mirror and support of one's own present and evolving existence and individuality.[66] The other is not only a necessary instrument of this process, but an indispensable part of it. *The other's* perception and condition are crucial to the friendship and to life. Children who witness their friends being accused or hurt, neglected or treated unfairly at school are often more upset than if they were objects of injustice themselves. "The self grows beyond its boundaries.

The other's wellbeing becomes as important as one's own," as Theodor Lidz wrote.[67] Hans Müller-Wiedemann referred to the theologian Schleiermacher, who said that "love always wants to make one out of two, while friendship wants to make two of everything."[68] The comradeship of the middle of childhood is real *friendship,* and very different from the highly dynamic love-relationships of youth and adult life. It possesses a special social element that lives in the modest, quiet respect for the other, for the friend who is different. This element will not return in later life in this purity, but it will profoundly affect all future relationships. ("The ability and will to form friendships rely on that practice in the middle of childhood."[69]) The pedagogical value of friendships at that time must be recognized and fostered. They offer children far more potential for biographical experience and inner growth than what is generally advertised and propagated in the outside world. ("Faced with the manifold temptations of the 'edutainment' industry that is spreading like a disease, today's school children are struggling to find a legitimate way of overcoming their loneliness through friendship" (Müller-Wiedemann).[70]

*

The relationships with peers and adults that are established in the middle of childhood can be central aspects of an individual's destiny. Hermann Koepke described Dante's imaginary-real meetings with Beatrice in his ninth year, encounters that essentially inspired his "vita nova."[71] Koepke spoke also of the extraordinary childhood experiences of the physician and poet Hans Carossa, who, during a period of severe illness at that age, intensely experienced the presence of his former playmate, Eva.[72] The study of numerous biographies reveals that the process of I-awakening is often accompanied by a sense of destiny that can affect children deeply and remain with them throughout their lives. At the age of nine, half way through his first moon-node period, Heinrich Schliemann longingly anticipated his destiny when he decided to marry Minna, and to excavate Troy and the royal tombs of Mycenae with her.[73]

This longing, which often has no object, is a soul element that presents itself frequently in the middle of childhood ("I am at home, but I am always homesick"[74]) as a deep inner emotional awareness of one's own existence. Karl Jaspers spoke of the "wealth he had already received" and the "sense of distance" that accompanied the experience of something "unattainable that was still part of me." Could some of the soul stirrings that children experience at that age—often in the meeting with others—have their roots before birth,[75] when destiny decisions were taken for the future incarnation that now reverberate as images in the child's feeling life and are subtly perceived there for the first time? Schliemann's first longing for discovery was not yet the expression of an adolescent zest for action and conquest or of elaborate future plans. It was more like the memory of a destiny, a careful finding or re-finding of life intentions deep inside him. Rudolf Steiner wrote about his own encounter with monks near Vienna as a child:

> There was a monastery of the Order of the Most Holy Redeemer on the slope of the mountains. I often met the monks on my walks. I still remember how glad it would have made me if they had spoken to me, but they never did. As a result, those meetings always left me with a somewhat vague but very solemn impression that remained for some time.
>
> It was in my ninth year when I became convinced that there were very important matters connected with the tasks of those monks, and that I had to learn what they were.[76]

Rudolf Steiner could only partly pursue his longing at the time; but it continued to live in his soul and remained part of him, of his individuality and biography.[77] At around the same time, he discovered geometry with the help of a revered assistant teacher, which was an experience that was deeply meaningful for him:

I derived a deep feeling of contentment from the fact that one could live with the soul in building forms that are seen wholly inwardly, independent of the outer senses. I found consolation for my mood caused by so many unanswered questions. The ability to grasp something purely through the spirit brought me an inner joy. I realize that I first knew happiness through geometry. [...] I would have said that the objects and events seen by the senses exist in space, the space outside the human being; but a kind of soul-space exists within as the setting for spiritual beings and events.[78]

"Me, I'm myself / No one in this big / world is like me / I'm different from you / and everyone else." As inner and outer conditions change dramatically at this "developmental moment"[79] and "turning point in life"[80] that will result in deepened self-awareness, children experience their I in a new way and sometimes sense what destiny holds in store for them. But these experiences remain in the sphere of moods or premonitions. As part of the incarnating process and of the biography, the soul has found a new orientation.

*

2.

MATURITY OF BREATHING

The middle of childhood
as part of the incarnating process

It is a time when we have the opportunity
to observe in what a wonderful way the forces
of the individuality unfold.

Rudolf Steiner[81]

IN HIS CONTRIBUTIONS to anthropology, Rudolf Steiner described in great detail the step children take in their development of body, soul and spirit during the second seven-year period. He referred in particular to the general changes that become apparent in the physical constitution and how they relate to the development of soul and spirit after the change of teeth has taken place. Rudolf Steiner did not see the second dentition as a localized event but as a "metamorphosis of life,"[82] the outer expression of the fact that the formative principle of the first seven years had come to completion.[83]

Up to that point, the child's organism was dominated by formative and constitutive processes that worked from the head down in close relation with the soul forces. Rudolf Steiner said the soul was "bound to the body" in early infancy, and that it was typical of young children to experience body and soul as one.[84] In the first seven years, physical phenomena are much closer to the soul processes than later. When young children eat, they devote themselves wholly, with "physical religiosity" (Steiner), to this process, which involves not just the body but their entire being. It is the same with sense impressions. They are not restricted to the body's periphery and the sense organs but permeate body and soul, which are both open and exposed to them, ready to imitate what they perceive. The situation changes at the end of the first seven years. The sense organs grow more independent and come to the surface. They emancipate themselves from the rest of the organism and "go their separate ways."[85] This is an essential process as it allows the former unity of body and soul to dissolve gradually. The child's soul can now "come into its own."[86] "It means that soul and spirit free themselves from the physical body, and children can unfold their own inner essence."[87] Up to this point, children were "all sense organ," devoted to and imitating their surroundings. Now they are "all soul."[88] With the second seven-year period a new stage of earthly life begins, and in the course of that stage the individuality will come to express itself in a special way.

In a lecture on curative education Rudolf Steiner described "in what a wonderful way the forces of the individuality unfold" at that time.[89] Many of the forces that previously supported the constitution and organization of the physical body are now freed for other tasks, such as learning. The child has attained school maturity.

During the second seven years "the development of life forces" takes over from the "formative processes" as the central element of the incarnating process.[90] The child's etheric life body begins to relate to the physical body in a different way, while the I, the child's individuality, becomes more "anchored" within this living organism.[91] The rhythmic system, which finds expression mostly in respiration and blood circulation, is now the central physiological aspect in the child's life. The activities of body and soul that characterize the second seven years radiate out from this system.[92] Rudolf Steiner said in a lecture about anthroposophy:

> It is the brain that is most active [in young children]! From the brain's activity, which is most pronounced up to the change of teeth, the sculpting forces radiate out into the entire body. After that, this formative activity is transferred to the respiration-heart system, where it remains till puberty.[93]

In the first seven years the neurosensory activity was dominant: what children took in from their surroundings, what
they imitated, internalized, and transformed ("incorporated")
into their own formative principles. The head with its essential
neurosensory functions was of central importance, with formative forces radiating out from it into the body.[94] At the end of
this period the leading physiological processes are transferred to
another location where they begin to work in a different way.
Rudolf Steiner elaborated on this change in a lecture to teachers,
given in Dornach on December 31, 1921:

> An important and far-reaching change is taking place
> when children begin to shed their milk teeth. This change
> is not only a physical event since the entire human organi-
> zation undergoes a metamorphosis. A true art of education
> demands a thorough appreciation and understanding of
> this metamorphosis. What in our previous meetings I have
> called the etheric body, or the refined body of formative
> forces, is freed from certain of its functions during the time
> between the change of teeth and puberty. Previously the
> etheric body was working directly into the physical body,
> but now it begins to function also in the child's soul. As a
> result of this the child's physical body is taken hold of from
> within in quite a different manner from that of the previous
> stage. Previously, the situation was more or less as mate-
> rialists—who see physical processes as the foundations of
> our soul life—would describe it. For them, soul and spirit
> are something that emanates from and is related to the
> body much as the candle flame is related to the candle.
> This might apply to young children up to the change of
> teeth. During these early years, the life of soul and spirit is
> entirely bound up with the child's physical and organic pro-
> cesses, and all physical and organic processes are reflected
> in the life of soul and spirit. All the shaping and forming
> of the body that is going on at that age is conducted from

the head downward. This stage finds its conclusion when the second teeth are being pushed through. At that time the forces working in the head cease to predominate, while the activities of soul and spirit enter the lower regions of the body, namely the rhythmical activities of heart and breathing. Previously, these forces, working especially upon the formation of the child's brain, also streamed down into the remaining organism, shaping and molding, and entering directly into the physical substances of the body, where they brought about physical processes.

All this changes when the second teeth appear, when certain of these forces begin to work more in the child's soul and spirit, and affect especially the rhythmic movement of heart and lungs. These forces are no longer active to the same degree in the physical processes, but begin to work also in the rhythms of breathing and blood circulation.[95]

The central rhythmic forces grow more intense ("with the breathing rhythm and the pulse of the blood gaining strength"). They will ultimately prevail over the previously dominant head organization.[96] What children experience in their life rhythms in the second seven-year period will have an essential effect on the "development of life forces" that is in itself harmonious. "The rhythm of breathing, the rhythm of the blood—the period between the change of teeth and puberty is governed by rhythm. Just rhythm!"[97]

We are not dealing here with a separate process that takes place in the hidden depths of the child's inner life, but an element of the child's ongoing participation in the events of the surrounding world. During the first seven years, the soul (and consequently the body also) used to live outside its boundaries, devoted to others, imitating, sharing, and internalizing their existence. The development of the rhythmic system is also influenced by the surroundings, but the influence is now transmitted by the breathing, with the soul being engaged in the process more freely. Rudolf Steiner wrote in a notebook:

> With the change of teeth, rhythm takes over. Children now give themselves fully to their surroundings and to their life of soul and spirit, absorbing impressions readily and with feeling. The chest organization develops under the influence of the environment.[99]

*

In regard to this evolving "chest organization," we need to bear in mind that, physiologically, the breathing is related to and oriented toward the neurosensory processes (and therefore the head organization), while the processes and rhythms of the blood are close to metabolism and the limbs.[100] When the rhythmic system of breathing and circulation rises to the center of the organic life processes, the different rhythmic processes have to find their own balance. Because of the overall predominance of the head organization (or neurosensory system), the breathing processes have greater functional impact up to the middle of childhood than the rhythms of the blood. After that, they will come closer to the circulation, "integrating themselves into it,"[101] which means that an individual equilibrium is established. *"A balance is established, a relationship between pulse and breathing that suits the individual person."*[102] The balance is found or established in the middle of childhood, at a time when powerful changes take place within the soul life. In a lecture that Rudolf Steiner gave to teachers in Dornach on April 17, 1923, he said:

> How breathing and blood circulation find an inner harmony, how children breathe at school, and how the breathing gradually adapts to the blood circulation, all that happens usually between the ninth and tenth year. Up

to the ninth year the breathing predominates. Then, the organism goes through an inner struggle, and a kind of harmony is established between the pulse and breathing. After that the blood circulation prevails. This will find its reflection in the body as well as in the soul.[103]

Rudolf Steiner did not elaborate on the subject in this instance, but he referred to a "transformation" of forces ("this transformation of forces at the meeting point between breathing and blood circulation is particularly significant."[104]) Elsewhere he said: "Between the ninth and tenth year lies the point in life when what was previously an element of breathing and used to be anchored in the upper human being, passes to the blood circulation; when the remarkable ratio of one to four emerges within the child, of approximately eighteen breaths to seventy-two pulses per minute."[105] Rudolf Steiner pointed out that this process of establishing a rhythm or balance is a "struggle" or crisis between breathing and blood circulation (and indirectly between neurosensory system and metabolism-limb-system, or between the upper and lower organism). ("Then, the organism goes through an inner struggle and a kind of harmony is established between pulse and breathing.") A new balance is sought and found in the process of incarnation, in the tension between heaven and earth, between cosmic head forces and processes and earthly limb forces and processes.[106] The "maturity of breathing" that develops in the second seven-year period precedes the "earth maturity" that will have to be attained in adolescence, and it relies on the "maturity of the senses" having been gained in early infancy.[107] Rudolf Steiner's picture for this process was that the rhythms of breathing and circulation (or, at another level, of astral and etheric body) "were storming at each other:"

At that time in life the etheric body, which passes through its own particular organizations before puberty, fights against the astral body. The child is confronted with an actual fight. If we look for the physical equivalent of this fight we can say: a real struggle takes place between the forces of growth and the forces we inhale when we breathe. This inner process is crucial and we need to study it increasingly if we really want to understand the human being.[108]

The "astral" or "soul body" is closely linked to the (cosmic) breathing processes of the upper human being, while the "etheric" life body is linked to the rising (earthly) blood processes that grow stronger in the middle of childhood. "The child is confronted with an actual fight." The crisis of the ninth or tenth year, which evolves as part of this process, has far-reaching consequences for the child's life [109] and, importantly, involves the heart organ.[110] Rudolf Steiner explained the physiological and functional processes we observe in children of that age as being the physical manifestation of dramatic inner changes. ("They find their physical expression at this point in life in the proper integration of the breathing and the blood circulation. A balance is found, a relationship between the pulse and breathing that suits the individual child. That is the physical manifestation [of the inner changes]; in their soul life and in their spiritual life, children now need us as teachers and educators."[111]) The physiological processes are merely "expressions of deep inner processes," as Steiner stated elsewhere."[112] Ultimately, both the physiological processes and changes and those of the inner soul life indicate a crisis of incarnation. In the course of that crisis children need to find a new balance that is appropriate to their age. Rudolf Steiner spoke in-depth about this in his lectures to physicians when he described the same process as the "integration of the individuality into the human organism from below." It is a process that turns against the dominance of head and senses, or against the I that is streaming in from above; and it comes with profound changes in the nutritional process, the warmth development, and the relationship of forces in general.[113] According to Steiner, the special balance and harmony of the second seven-year period is entirely due to the augmentation of the stream "from below" that prepares the child for earthly maturity: "Only now [in the middle of childhood] does the tool of the individuality, polarity—that is, the interaction of our lower and higher aspects—find the right balance...."[114]

*

In the course of their second seven years, children find their rhythmic center in a conflict that allows them to establish a new inner equilibrium. This is a physiological process that does not take place only in the soul life but also in the encounter between the individuality and the world, and with the help of its forces: "The child's development proceeds from breathing and circulation. *The child is wholly listener and musician.*"[115] In the middle of childhood our individuality is particularly sensitive to what lives musically and artistically in the structures we find and absorb. Rudolf Steiner said to the teachers:

> Just think of how everything musical is related to the rhythmic system. Music is nothing but rhythm carried into the human rhythmic system. The inner human being becomes a lyre or violin. One's whole rhythmic system reproduces what the violin or piano has played. And, as it is with music, so it is in a finer, more delicate way with modeling and painting. Color harmonies and melodies are also reproduced and live in us as inner rhythmic processes.[116]

Although Rudolf Steiner most often used music to demonstrate the activity of the constitutive forces in and around children of that age, he emphasized in some instances the significance of other artistic experiences that also possess an inner rhythm and musicality. The children's life forces focus on musical qualities,[117] on what lives in language and in music without being restricted to either.[118] In Stuttgart, on October 16, 1920, he explained:

> They are forces of a musical nature that we take up from the outer world, the world outside us, from our observation of nature and its processes, above all from our observation of nature's regularities and irregularities. Because everything going on in nature is permeated by a hidden music, the earthly projection of the "music of the spheres," every plant, every animal actually incorporates a tone of the music of the spheres. This is also true of the human body: the music of the spheres still lives in the forms and structure of the body, although it no longer lives in our speech as an expression of our soul life. Children absorb all this unconsciously, and they are therefore so highly musical. They take all of this into their bodily organism.[119]

Children meet the rhythm and music inherent in the world unconsciously or semi-consciously, and they receive through it essential inspiration for their physiological task of harmonizing their breathing and pulse as a basis for the subsequent shaping of the physical body. Children absorb what is musical in the outer world and transform it into inner formative forces even *before* they reach the turning point of the ninth or tenth year: "When we see how children up to that time between the ninth and tenth year absorb the musical element, how the sculpting effect of music is absorbed naturally by the body's inner plasticity, and how readily the musical element is transformed into dance-like movement, we realize that children do not take hold inwardly of the musical element until they have reached the ninth or tenth year. It is quite obvious."[120] The rhythmic center must be fully developed or, in other words, breathing and circulation must be balanced before children can "take hold inwardly of the musical element." For only then will they have prepared the necessary physical conditions. ("Only from the ninth year and up to the age of twelve will children develop an understanding of rhythm and beat as such, of the melodious element as such. Then, they no longer want to reproduce rhythm and beat inwardly but perceive them as separate structures outside them. While they experienced rhythm and beat before, it is only now that they begin to understand them."[121]) Especially in the time between the change of teeth and the turning point of the ninth or tenth year, when the rhythmic balance is established, children internalize the musical structures of their surroundings. It is a physiological process that belongs to this part of childhood and that will continue, more or less intensely, until earth maturity has been attained: "If we say that children up to their seventh year are inwardly sculptors, we must add that up to their fourteenth year, up to puberty, they are inwardly musicians."[122] Children will not gain a true understanding of musical laws and forces until they have found their rhythmic balance. Before and after that they use these forces to build up their body.

The musical element that children perceive in and absorb from the world around them "vibrates through" their soul body,[123] stimulating body and soul into immediate activity. ("They vibrate too. They reproduce inwardly what they perceive outside.[124]) Children need rhythm and music now. They "want their bodies to be permeated by musical rhythms," as Rudolf Steiner explained in a lecture to teachers:

> Children of that age feel a strong inner urge to experience their evolving inner life of soul and spirit, but in an unconscious, instinctive way, as rhythm and beat. They long for this rhythm and beat to manifest *within their organization*. Everything we bring to children after the change of

teeth must be presented in a way that allows children to incorporate it into their intentions. If we want to be artists as teachers we must be able to live in a pulsating, rhythmical element, which speaks to children and gives them the feeling that they are in their element.[125]

Children long for a rhythmical musical element, they long to be surrounded by music because the musical element corresponds to their inner life and allows them to develop and shape their body inwardly "as musicians."[126] According to Rudolf Steiner children perceive, imitate and internalize the musicality of their surroundings intensely also in the first seven years. Before the second dentition these musical impressions were transformed into sculptural forces, now they can be transformed into "inner musicality."

When he spoke of the importance of this process for the constitution of the physical body, Rudolf Steiner mentioned in particular the thorough organization of the muscular (later also the skeletal) system through the forces that the rhythmic system absorbed, transformed, and integrated into the organism: "In the early years of childhood, up to the completed ninth year, children want to experience everything that comes toward them as inner rhythm and beat. What comes from the outside *can then become one with the child's breathing and heartbeat and can, indirectly, work into the shaping of muscles and bones.*"[127] On December 31, 1921, in Dornach, Rudolf Steiner said to the teachers:

> Since the ether body works differently now, it is primarily the limbs that grow at this age. The life of the muscles and bones has a particular part to play now, trying to adapt to the life of the breathing and the pulse. The muscles vibrate quite strongly with the rhythms of the breathing and pulse, and the child's entire being wants to become musical.[128]

In fact, it is mostly the muscular system that is organized musically through the rhythmic system of the middle, once that system has found its balance: "When children are almost ten years old, the rhythms of blood and breathing begin to develop and flow more into the muscular system. The muscles become saturated with blood, and the blood pulses through the muscles in intimate response to our inner human nature and the heart. Between the ages of ten and twelve we build up our rhythmic system in correspondence to our inner disposition."[129] The muscles are "intimately connected to the system of respiration and blood circulation, and in tune with it." Imbued with the internal rhythm, the children's movements become more harmonious and natural:

> If we observe children with real insight, we notice that from the ninth to tenth year children process soul experiences by involving the growth forces of the muscular system. At that time of life the more intimate growth forces of the muscular system are always taking part in the soul life. The inner growing or stretching of muscles depends essentially on the development of the soul forces.
>
> It is characteristic of this age between ten and twelve that the muscles are intimately connected to the system of respiration and blood circulation, and in tune with it. A truly artistic education will respond to this. Through the breathing and the pulse we work on the muscular system.[130]

When the child is almost twelve and approaches earthly maturity, the muscles lose their intimate connection with the system of respiration and blood circulation, and begin to succumb to the mechanical forces of the skeletal system.[131] Now the process of integration into the outside world sets in with all the possibilities and challenges that are so particularly characteristic of adolescence.[132]

*

In the middle of childhood, children live entirely out of *their central forces*, out of their inner soul realm, which they enter with growing awareness from the age of nine or ten. Once a rhythmic balance has been achieved, the child's feeling life begins to change, including the relationship to language that is now no longer based on imitation, but becomes increasingly expressive of the child's individuality.[133] After the change of teeth, the sensitivity for language continues to grow. It is an important aspect of school maturity: "During the first seven years of their life, children are interested in gestures and movement; between seven and fourteen their interest is focused on everything pictorial. Language has wonderful pictorial qualities; thus, after the change of teeth their interest shifts from gestures to language."[134] There is no doubt that children enjoy and are interested in language also in the first seven years; but it is the active other person in the room, the adult, the brother or sister, who is important and whose actions and behaviors—not so much their words—are perceived and internalized. Through listening and imitation they grow into language.

Children in the first seven years conquer the space around them through their limbs and begin to orientate themselves in that space. But now, in the second seven-year period, the life process shifts to the center of the child's being. "Between the change of teeth and sexual maturity, children enter into a wholly different relationship to the spoken word."[135] Increasingly, they "wake up" to what others say and no longer only to what they do. Children experience that the individuality and inner essence, and also the morality, of the other person come to expression in their language. This means that as teachers we can now reach the children through the word.[136] "*Words and their meaning now give the child direction. Simply through the human individuality words and their meaning now give direction.*"[137]

This whole development unfolds against the background, and on the basis, of the processes that take place in the rhythmic system during the second seven-year period. Once children have reached their ninth or tenth year they are able to "feel their way into language."[138] This process and the newly emerging "sense of linguistic style"[139] have to do with the central rhythmic balance that they also help to bring about. There are striking accounts and poems from children of that age that bear testimony to this process of "feeling their way into the language." The faculty of children to remember experiences as well as experience feelings concerning such memories is supported by rhythmic processes: "With the right kind of observation we come to the conclusion that up to the change of teeth the inner activity that plays a part in memorizing, and that therefore lives in the memory, is now, more than later, like an outer habit that develops in the child's physical organization. Children remember and they remember well, but their remembering strikes us, quite rightly, as the repetition of actions that have been acquired as skills. The memory of children during the first developmental stage is, in fact, an inner skill, a developed inner habit. It is only after the change of teeth that children really look back with mental images on their experiences, in a kind of review. Their soul life changes drastically once they begin to remember."[140] After the change of teeth, experiences reappear as remembered concepts or mental images. Before the change of teeth, children live in habits that are not reflected in mental images.[141]

Children quite obviously take an important step forward on their way toward earthly maturity. Once adolescents have gained earthly maturity they are in full possession of their soul forces. After the initial stage of orientation toward space and actions, and the subsequent stage of penetrating language through feeling (in the middle of childhood), children now come closer to the thinking self that is able to form ideals and transform them into guidelines through will activity. The young person is now able to experience the coming together of thinking, feeling, and will activity. Unlike children in the middle of childhood, adolescents can be guided by ideals, by thoughts about their own self and their intentions; and they can act accordingly out of their own will.[142] However, they will only be able to do this if they bring with them from the middle of childhood, and, more specifically, from the crisis of the ninth and tenth year, the strong sense of self that is needed for the true individuality to unfold. Rudolf Steiner said about the importance of the child's relationship to language during the second seven-year period:

> All aspects of the soul that come to expression in language will move to another developmental stage and assume a different character. These processes are largely unconscious, but they determine the child's entire future development. Between the ages of seven and fourteen children struggle with what lives in their language—or languages if they happen to speak several. They are not aware of this struggle because it is unconscious. But they struggle because what emerges from their rhythmic system as sound now integrates itself more and more intensely into their thoughts, feelings, and will intentions. This struggle with the language shows that children begin to become aware of their own self.[143]

*

If, through age-appropriate education, the "internal musical structure" described by Rudolf Steiner can develop into a balanced relationship of respiration and blood circulation,[144] the rhythmic system will not only be established as the center of the child's physiological life, it will also optimize the development of the second seven-year period. If "maturity of breathing"—in harmony with the blood circulation—has been achieved, health-giving forces can stream through the body from the child's rhythmic center through the respiratory process (supported by the etheric body). *"Due to our inner make-up we are in fact most healthy at the second stage of life, between the second dentition and sexual maturity,"* Rudolf Steiner said to the physicians.[145] In a general anthroposophical lecture, he said:

> All healing forces originate in the respiratory system. We can know the healing forces that arise within us if we really understand our breathing. The other systems do not generate healing forces. They are themselves in need of healing. [...]. A mysterious healing activity arises from the respiratory system. All the mysteries of healing are indeed mysteries of respiration.[146]

The healthy breathing rhythm, which is established out of the body's own forces in the middle of childhood, is essentially different from what has been physically inherited from the parents.[147] It generates forces that are harmonizing and healing. The rhythmic system, which has its center in the breathing, does not grow tired and never becomes "over-excited" by its own inner activity.[148] Rudolf Steiner pointed out that the middle of childhood as such is the healthiest time of our life. Unhealthy influences and phenomena always come from the outside in the second seven-year period.[149]

In a lecture to teachers, Rudolf Steiner spoke about the physiognomy of children at that age and about how the rhythmic balance, once it is established, affects the further biography:

> If we teach artistically we will be able to observe that the physiognomy of the children really changes. We will notice subtle differences in their physical expression. Between the ages of seven and nine, children take hold of their inner life, and we can see that something healthily active—not nervously active—appears in their faces. It is of the foremost importance for the child's entire life that this happens. It is this appearance of a healthily-active moment

in their physiognomy that will enable children to love the world, to develop a feeling for the world in later life and inner healing forces to ward off any kind of hypochondria, unnecessary critical attitudes, etc.[150]

Rudolf Steiner spoke in great depth about the physiological and psychological changes in the middle of childhood because he was fully aware of the important part education and educators play in this important process of transition. Children do not automatically achieve the necessary balance of respiration and blood processes and all the possibilities that arise due to this balance. They need a suitable, supportive environment for this. It was important to Rudolf Steiner to prepare teachers and parents for their educational tasks and to develop a teaching method that can do justice to the specific requirements of this stage in child development.

*

3.

I and You

Waldorf Teaching and the pedagogical significance of the other person

> We have to attend to each individual child
> at this moment because it will affect
> the whole of his or her life.
>
> Rudolf Steiner[151]

As soon as children enter school they need to be taught in a way that corresponds to their inner forces. Teachers need to understand these forces and respond to them. Anthroposophically speaking, we need to address the forces that are set free at this age and that, up to the change of teeth, had actively built up the body to which they were bound. These ("etheric") forces available to the child "know" the formative principles, the body's morphology and functionality, since they were once involved in forming this body. If we want these forces to serve the child's learning, that is, the further development of the child's soul and spirit, we have to retain the bridge to the past and not change what we teach, but how we teach it. Rudolf Steiner said in a lecture: "That is why, in the Waldorf School, we introduce writing in a wholly artistic way. We do not teach children writing as such, but let them draw and paint basic forms so that, in this activity, they can bring to expression what has been released during the change of teeth. When children apply their hands and fingers in drawing and painting, we find that what used to weave in the soul realm is now projected into their whole being in accordance with its physical form. By bringing the child's hands and fingers into movement we allow the organizing principle that used to work in the soul realm to continue its activity. [...] We must always ensure that the forces of soul and spirit that have been liberated are employed in a way that is really appropriate for the growing child. We must 'copy' the forces in the soul and spirit realm that are trying to leave the physical organization, so that they can be employed rightly for the child's growth and development. We must know the human essence intimately and teach in a way that stimulates the child's inner harmonious being. We must draw everything out of the child's inner essence."[152] In order to achieve this, teachers must be artists and education must be an art. It is our task as teachers to make available to understanding and learning "the forces that had shaped the organism."[153] We need to know these forces well so that we can take hold of them in an artistic way.

In the second seven-year period the child's soul forces, which had been active in building up the body, also "strive toward vivid inward pictures,."[154] This is why we teach through pictures during the first school years. We also have to address and involve the physiological rhythmic system, which is now at the center of the incarnation process. When we attend to both these aspects we teach age-appropriately because it is due to the liberation of the etheric forces, and with their help, that the child's rhythmic system develops.[155] When we teach artistically through pictures and when our teaching content and method have an essentially musical structure,[156] we address the rhythmic system and its forces and nurture the child. ("When we are with children we should teach and behave in a way that allows them to unfold their rhythmic system freely and harmoniously."[157]) In Stuttgart, on June 22, 1922, Rudolf Steiner spoke about this to the teachers:

The rhythmic system [...] is stimulated directly by the soul when we teach artistically. It will soon become apparent that this way of teaching hardly tires the children. As teachers we must learn to notice when students are too tired, or that they have gotten tired from physical circumstances that affect the metabolism and the limb system, such as stale air in the classroom, or having to sit still for an excessively long time. The children have to think, after all. If thoughts reverberate quietly in the rhythmic system the children will not get too tired. The physical organ that needs to be addressed particularly by education is the rhythmic system. This means that with subjects that are not artistic in themselves we need to make more of an effort to teach them in as artistic a way as possible. This is something that we need to take very seriously because between the change of teeth and puberty the artistic approach is the only true means of education.[158]

Rudolf Steiner said elsewhere that one-sided intellectual teaching was harmful because it interfered with the healthy development of the rhythmic system:

If our teaching is too intellectual and not imaginative enough the child's breathing is disturbed in a delicate, subtle way. I would say that the child's breathing-out becomes congested. You have to imagine this as a very subtle and refined, not crude, process. The process of expiration becomes congested, and the child experiences something like a subconscious nightmare if the teaching is too intellectual between the seventh and the fourteenth year. A kind of inner, intimate nightmare comes into being that remains with the organism and leads in later life to asthmatic conditions or other diseases connected with a congested breathing process.[159]

Rudolf Steiner did not elaborate on the pathogenesis of particular diseases here, but intended to call attention to the real tasks of school education. The rhythmic system comes to the fore in the second seven-year period and needs to be treated appropriately. It needs an age-appropriate education that is attuned to the physiology and psychology of the growing child. Teaching methods and content based on abstract theories (as those of the state school curricula) that are not founded on anthropological considerations bring the body's functional processes into disorder. They affect the development of the child's personality and individuality in a serious way and can lead to physical illness or a disposition to such illness in later life.[160]

*

Rudolf Steiner pointed out that, with regard to teaching content, we need to bear in mind that the children's experience of their own self and of the world has not yet become separate before the dramatic change of the ninth or tenth year. In order to do justice to this, Rudolf Steiner asked and encouraged teachers to present the ensouled world in a pictorial way rather than force cognitive contents on children prematurely. —"We have to use the language of folktales; everything in the external world must still be one with the child. Plants have to speak to each other, kiss each other, have a mother and father, and so on."[161] "After the change of teeth, children will experience a conceptual way of thinking as if spikes were being driven through their whole being, especially if such concepts are taken from the inorganic or lifeless realm. Anything that is not ensouled will estrange the child. When we teach children of this age, we need the artistic ability of imbuing everything we bring to them with life. Everything must live. We must let plants speak. We must let animals act as moral beings. We must be able to turn the whole world into a folktale, into fables and legends."[162] "And I must underline [...] that it is the worst possible experience for a child before the end of the ninth or tenth year to be given a mechanical explanation of a train engine, a tram, or any other mechanical contrivance."[163]

Only from the turning point in the middle of childhood are children really able "to understand nature as such"[164] and to "approach plants and animals in a realistic way."[165] It is certainly possible to bring "realistic" knowledge to children before then, to teach them and ask them to reproduce such knowledge cognitively. But such an approach is not attuned to the child's development and causes subtle disintegration processes. The soul forces are activated prematurely and lose their connection with the personality as a whole and with the world. Although there is general pressure in our culture to teach in that way, it is an approach that Rudolf Steiner rejected. He pleaded that we do justice to the mood and state of consciousness of children in their seventh or eighth year (and to their unconscious *longing*) by adjusting our presentations accordingly, and that we pay attention to the crucial turning point that marks the middle of childhood. He asked for a renewal of what we teach and of the way we teach: "Their sense of self allows children now to have a relationship with nature and with their environment that makes it possible for us to speak to them about how things and processes relate *to one another*. Before, they were mostly interested in how things and processes relate to *human beings*."[166]

According to Rudolf Steiner, the change described means that we have a particular task as teachers. The successful establishment of the rhythmic system and the newly emerging "sense of self" allow us to speak about "things and processes" as separate from us or from the child ("speak to them more about how things and processes relate *to one another*"). At the same time we must ensure that the process of separation does not result in alienation, that the I does not feel alone or separate from the world. Starting from the crisis around the ninth year we can speak to children "*more* about how things and processes relate to one another," but, in doing so, we must never lose sight of the important relationship of the individual with the world and the relationship of nature with the human being. Rudolf Steiner spoke emphatically to the teachers about the importance of helping children, once they have reached self-awareness, to gain an "understanding of the plant world based on feeling"[167] and to bring to life in them the experience that each plant is part of the earth's organism and that it is the "living earth that brings forth plants."[168] "Presenting children with plants that were torn from the earth is a horrible thing to do."[169] We must allow children to experience the plant in relation to the earth's organism. Instead of separating and analyzing the mortal plant individuality ("the poor tree...") we must awaken an understanding of the "real world" of which the plant is an integral part. In August 1924, Rudolf Steiner said to the teachers in Torquay:

> [...] If you show children plants out of a botanist's box and simply announce their names, you will be teaching something quite unreal. This will have consequences for the rest of their life, for this kind of plant knowledge will never give them an understanding of how the soil must be cared for and fertilized, or of how it receives life forces with the manure. Children can only gain an understanding of how to cultivate the land if they know how the soil is really part of the plant. People today understand reality less and less [...] and therefore look at everything in isolation. [...] In order to understand how the earth is really a part of plant life we must find out what kind of soil each plant belongs to; we can learn about manure only if we consider the earth and the plant world as a unity, and if we see the earth as an organism and the plant as something that grows in this organism.
>
> If we do this, children will feel, from the very start, that the earth they are standing on is alive, which is crucial for their whole future.[170]

With this approach (that Rudolf Steiner described in various lectures on education) we enable children to reconnect with the world consciously and lovingly once their sense of self has become independent after the middle of childhood. Children who are taught about plants and soil in this way will experience that "the earth they are standing on is alive"—despite the impressions of temporality and finality that surge up in their

inner being—because they benefit from an *"enlivening* education," which as Steiner pointed out is particularly relevant in
the second seven-year period. ("Bring life to the young children
because their etheric bodies have been entrusted to you.")[171]

As with the plants, we also have to demonstrate how the
animal kingdom relates to the human world, based on special
features and soul qualities of animals. In Torquay, Rudolf Steiner
said:

> Looking at the different kinds of animals that live on
> the earth and their soul qualities, we find there are fierce
> predators, gentle lambs, and also courageous animals.
> Some birds and mammals are very brave fighters. We find
> majestic beasts like the lion. We find the various soul quali-
> ties in the animals, and we see them as characteristic of
> this or that species. We call the tiger fierce, since fierceness
> is its foremost quality. We call the sheep patient, because
> that is its most important quality. We call the donkey
> lazy, because there is something very lazy about a donkey,
> although it might not actually be all that lazy. A donkey is
> certainly reluctant to move, and if set on walking slowly,
> there is nothing that can induce it to walk quickly. And so
> every animal has its own particular characteristics.
>
> But we cannot think about people in this way. We cannot
> think of one person as being only gentle and patient,
> another only fierce, and a third only brave. We would find
> it very one-sided if people were spread across the earth
> in this way. Even though there can be a prevalence of a
> particular quality in some people, it is not as strong as in
> animals. What we must do with human beings, especially
> if it is our task to educate them, is teach them patience in
> certain situations, and courage, even fierceness, in others.
> Although there are situations or facts to which people nat-
> urally may react with a certain ferocity, this should, how-
> ever, be administered homeopathically.

Let us look more closely at these soul qualities in us and in the animals. As human beings we can possess all these qualities that the animals have among them, with each animal possessing a different one. We can have a little of each. We cannot be as majestic as the lion, but we have something majestic in us. We are not as fierce as tigers, but we have an element of fierceness. We are not as patient as the sheep, but we have some patience. We are not as lazy as the donkey—not all of us are—but we have an amount of laziness in us. Everybody has. If we look at it rightly, we have to say that we combine something of the lion, of the sheep, of the tiger, and of the donkey within us, but in a certain harmony: the different qualities balance each other. We are the synthesis of the different animal soul qualities. We will achieve the right balance if the right amount of all these animal qualities is introduced into our nature.

There is a beautiful old Greek proverb that says: If courage be united with cleverness it will bring you blessing, but if it goes alone ruin will follow. If we were only courageous like some birds, but fought continuously, we would not bring much blessing to our life. As human beings we need to achieve the right combination of cleverness and courage.

With us there needs to be a synthesis, a harmony of everything that is spread out in the animal kingdom [...] The animal kingdom is a spread out human being, the human being is the animal kingdom in contraction. All animals are synthesized in the human being, and if we analyze the human being we find the whole animal kingdom. [...] We also find in our organs, outwardly, a milder, harmonized reflection of the different animal qualities. Everything that is found in the animal world, even in the shapes of animals, is also present in the human being. This is how we learn what our true relationship is with the animal world, how all animals taken together make up a human being.[172]

With this approach to teaching, we can bring the nature realms as part of the living earth and of humanity back to the children after they have lost their natural oneness with the world. This is very important for their understanding of themselves and of the world:

> If we enliven our teaching about animals and plants in this way, by giving individual examples, we also show how we as human beings relate to the world inwardly. The children can then grow into the world in the right way at a time when they are learning to differentiate between subject and object. By studying the plants we will be able to separate the world from the human being, while at the same time building a bridge from the human being to the world; the bridge that needs to be there if the right feeling, the right love for the world is to develop.[173]

> We will then stand on the earth in the right way and have the right relationship to it. It is essential that we achieve this with our teaching.[174]

It is a matter of conveying to children a sense of the important position we have as human beings in the general world order,[175] not in order to encourage a feeling of arrogance or hubris but rather in order to cultivate a sense of our position, character and task in the cosmos (spiritually as well as ecologically). Later, adolescents can experience the will dimension of this task.

*

Rudolf Steiner developed a method not only for natural history teaching, but also for language and grammar (he often emphasized the significance of these subjects for an age-appropriate development of I-awareness),[176] as well as for history, religion,[177] and many other subjects. In doing so, he brought particular attention to the tasks and challenges confronting the various age-groups and to the overall goal of Waldorf education, that is, the nurturing of the child's *"life force."*[178] He gave the following example for teaching history in the middle of childhood:

> It is futile to try to teach history to children before they are nine or ten. They will have no understanding of it. However, once they are nine or ten (you can observe this for yourself), they begin to be interested in individual personalities. When you portray *Caesar, Achilles, Hector, Agamemnon,* or *Alcibiades,* simply, as individuals, keeping the whole historical context in the background, you will find that the children are really interested. They will even be eager to find out more. Give them pictures that are complete in themselves. Give them vivid descriptions of what a meal would have been like in the various centuries, how people ate before forks were invented, what a meal was like in ancient Rome. Describe how Classical Greek people walked, how with each step they were aware of the form of their legs. Describe how the Hebrew people of the Old Testament walked, with no sense of form, letting their arms dangle loosely. We teach history in the right way to ten- to twelve-year-olds if we invoke feelings for these details that we present in pictures.[159]
>
> It is only after that, that we can move on to the historical context. Only then will children be able to understand the concept of cause and effect, and history as such can be taught [...][179]

Not until children become aware of themselves, of their own inner space and life story, from the ninth or tenth year, do they "begin to be interested in individuals" (historical or contemporary) and understand them as individualities with their own inner life who perform actions in history. With the awakening self-awareness in the physiological and psychological crisis of the ninth year and the related development of the rhythmic system, children gain the ability to perceive the I of the other person. The emerging relationship with their own life story brings with it the possibility of understanding the history of the world in general, based on individual figures who were active in history. Just as, from the age of nine or ten, nature studies are meant to support children in finding their roots in their natural environment in a new and conscious way, the history lessons with their biographical and cultural narratives will help to establish a relationship with time that goes beyond their own biography and allows the children to see themselves as part of a wider community. History as a subject becomes educational, for, in their attempt to feel themselves into historical processes, the children experience examples of successful (or failing) existences to which they can orientate themselves. The subject does not only provide (examinable) historical "knowledge," it offers essential support in the children's search for and confirmation of their own identity. *"We must no longer even think that subjects are there to be taught. We must be clear about the fact that, from the seventh to the fourteenth year, thinking, feeling, and the will have to be developed in the right way in children. Geography, mathematics—all the subjects aid the appropriate development of thinking, feeling, and the will."*[180]

*

While attaching much value to the methods and contents of Waldorf teaching, to age-appropriateness and differentiation, Rudolf Steiner left no doubt whatsoever that the personality of the teacher and the teacher's relationship with the children was of the utmost importance. Teaching methods and subjects do not work as such but through the personalities involved and the pedagogical relationship. There is no such thing as successful Waldorf education without the personality of the teacher. Especially at the time of the "silent" crisis of the ninth or tenth year, the educator is, as Rudolf Steiner emphasized, the immensely important "other person" to whom the children can relate: they "appeal for help [to the teacher] not by asking outright questions, but through their behavior."[181]

Rudolf Steiner expected (and strongly urged) that Waldorf teachers form a strong relationship with the children in their care.[182] When the first Waldorf school was founded in Stuttgart, he pointed out in his opening address of September 7, 1919: "[...] As educators we need to awaken in ourselves a living human nature that is able to experience inwardly the child's entire being by entering into a spiritual relationship with the child."[183] Teachers should strive to understand the human being "at the deepest level" and meet the children "with the love that grows from such an inner attitude," Steiner said in a later course on education.[184] A "spiritual-physiological way of teaching"[185] had to be developed, that would grow out of the knowledge of and love for human nature. We should see Rudolf Steiner's detailed descriptions of the middle of childhood and the crisis of the ninth or tenth year against this background: gaining true knowledge of human beings that allows for an age-appropriate, "spiritual-physiological way of teaching" and opens up the space for a suitable relationship.

*

Again and again, Rudolf Steiner explained that children, from when the time they start school, actively *seek* the pedagogical relationship with their teacher. Their "life of imitation" of the first seven years changes after the second dentition to a life in which it is "their natural instinct to follow authority."[186] In a public lecture on the "Fundamentals of Waldorf Education," given in the Swiss town of Aarau in 1921, Rudolf Steiner said:

The forces that make children imitators to such an extent that they imitate even the slightest hand movement, emerge around the age of seven as the liberated forces that educators and teachers have to address. Looking more closely at this development, one recognizes that, while children are compulsive imitators up to the age of seven, they need to experience a natural sense of authority during the next seven years up to puberty and to accept the teacher as their rightful guide on life's path. The experience of authority becomes the main educational principle for children between the change of teeth and puberty.[187]

From the moment children enter school, their relationship with the teacher can no longer be based primarily on imitation, but needs to be built increasingly on the children's active interest in the lesson. With the second seven-year period children enter the sphere of the word in a new and increasingly conscious manner, out of the forces of the rhythmic system. They become listeners who no longer need to imitate life around them actively: "While the children before [...] simply accepted and imitated what was going on around them, whether good or bad, right or wrong, they no longer feel the urge to imitate after the change of teeth. They now listen to hear from the world what they ought and ought not to do."[188] In the second seven-year period, from the change of teeth to puberty, children "listen intensely to the people around them."[189] They long to be guided by role-models, especially through the spoken word. "It is the word with its meaning that gives direction now. Simply through a person's essence, the word with its meaning gives direction now."[190] "Before that, the eye was keen to imitate, the ear was keen to imitate. Now children begin to listen to what comes from adults as their opinion or their view. The drive to imitate is transformed into devotion to the authority."[191]

The children still rely on the forces of *devotion* and *trust*. The readiness and capacity to imitate in the first seven years was fed by these forces that now also appear—in a metamorphosed form—in the relationship with the teacher, in the trustful looking up to the teacher as the authority whose word carries weight and sets standards.

Rudolf Steiner never promoted authority and obedience as virtues in support of leadership and order or as a preparation for an authoritarian social order or regime. Instead, he emphasized the anthropological fact that children after the change of teeth long for another person whose views are important to them. Steiner spoke of an "absolute devotion to the teacher"[192] as a freely chosen authority. Children do, of course, not chose which teacher they will have. But the feelings they bring toward their teacher come out of their own inner being, out of the inner forces at work at that age. *"We thoroughly misunderstand human nature if we fail to realize that the longing to have an authority next to them is a fundamental force and sentiment of children from the age of six or seven to fourteen or fifteen."*[193] In the second seven-year period the principle of authority is the "most essential principle in education," the "most essential power in education."[194] Rudolf Steiner pointed out that it is a principle that needs to find more and more consideration in the future.[195]

With the publishing of *Philosophy of Freedom* in his thirty-third year, Rudolf Steiner began building his entire life and work on the idea of freedom in the age of Michael.[196] Gaining the capacity for freedom, which he defined as the capacity to motivate our actions through ideas that we have fully understood and accepted, was for him *the* object of education, an "education toward freedom." Children are free by nature. It is in their orientation to the teacher that they gain (in body, soul and spirit) the foundations that will allow them in later life, in adolescence, to form individual judgments and act in accordance with them. On February 27, 1921, in The Hague, Rudolf Steiner said:

> Just as the earlier need to play resurfaces at around the age of twenty as a greater or lesser ability to cope with life, a similar transformation takes place with regard to the child's reverence for the teacher as a figure of authority.

The trust in the authority of adults has to be able to fully unfold between the ages of seven and fifteen so that the young person can develop the right sense of freedom as a foundation for social skills in later life. We cannot be free as adults if we have not experienced a relationship of authority as children. And we cannot feel love for others later in the social sphere, if we have not had the possibility to adjust to our environment through imitation in early childhood. We don't need imitation in later life, but we need social awareness. This depends on whether the children had teachers or educators in the first seven year's of their life that were worthy of imitation. We need individuals who take hold of their life out of a strong sense of freedom. They are the ones who were able to experience a natural authority in their teacher or educator between the change of teeth and puberty.[197]

As teachers we need to meet the children's inner "longing" for a guiding personality[198] through a relationship that the children *seek* and that the teacher *provides* in selfless love. This relationship can form the foundation for teaching and transmitting knowledge. For Rudolf Steiner it was not the lesson content (the word) that was of primary importance, but the relationship with the child—as the foundation for everything that was to come: "It is of great importance for growing children that they can accept something as their thought, that they can live into something *because* the revered adult has expressed this thought or this sentiment—because the developing person and the adult are growing together."[199] As teachers we should meet the children, who look up to us with trust and reverence, with our true self, our true personality, our "humanity"[200]—not with severity and punishment ("we should meet the children naturally, through what we are."[201]) Then we can become a "gateway to the world"[202] for the children, a mediator and "representative"[203] of the world. It is *through* the teacher that the children meet the knowledge of the world (the knowledge of natural history, mathematics, geography and history, language, the arts and religion). Teachers "represent" the knowledge of the world, and therefore the world, to the children. Rudolf Steiner pointed out that children do not need to "understand" or comprehend all the content that is brought to them in the first years of school. There are things that they just listen to and internalize because they trust their beloved teacher ("taken into the soul through love, through the love that is the most important educational principle."[204]) These things may be understood fully only in later life. This pedagogical principle was extremely important for Rudolf Steiner and he repeatedly and emphatically referred to it, even though it went against the demands of a time that extolled a decidedly cognitive approach. ("It is extremely important for us to have moments in our life, at the age of 30 or 40, when we can say: now I understand something that I accepted on authority in my eighth or ninth year or even earlier. — *That is enlivening.*"[205])

*

Rudolf Steiner also stressed to educators and teachers the importance of moral development in the second seven-year period. Again, he was not talking about "doctrines", "orders" and "interdictions", about maxims and reflections, but about the sympathies and antipathies that we awaken in the children through our personalities and through our teaching. "Children need to receive the world instinctively through the feeling they have for their teachers, so that they develop through their sympathies and antipathies a sense of 'this is good, this is evil'. They need to take in the world *through us*. Children will benefit from being able to form their first relationship with the world through the mediation of the teacher."[206] Steiner placed great value on the aesthetic element. When children establish the balance of their rhythmic system during the second seven-year period, a "sense of beauty" is born in them.[207] As teachers we have to work with this sense of beauty, not by creating the illusion that there is an ideal world without evil, but by building on the central forces of balance. Once children cease to imitate what they perceive because the forces of imitation, the "sense" of imitation decreases, we need to support them in learning to "reproduce the outside world *in a beautiful way*."[208] In nurturing and realizing this "sense of beauty" through an artistic approach to teaching we develop the children's "inner aesthetic sense of pleasure and displeasure also in the moral realm." "At the beginning we must not preach what is moral and forbid what is immoral [...]. It is in the *feeling*, not in the will, that we must, between the change of teeth and puberty, foster a sense for what is good and what is evil. We must be inwardly pleased with what is good. We must develop love and sympathy for what is good before it becomes a duty (in adolescence). Moral will intentions have to grow out of the moral feeling of pleasure and disgust."[209] "Children are *pleased* about what is good if we bring it to them in the right way through our example."[210] Rudolf Steiner referred to children in the second seven-year period as "aestheticians."[211] If the right conditions prevail, children find a profound inner harmony in the musicality of their rhythmic system. This rhythmic system is an organ for the perception of what is beautiful and right (or ugly and wrong) in their surroundings. If we teach in the right way this perception can grow into "pleasure" at what is good and "displeasure" at what is evil. Children in the middle of childhood need neither reflections on morality nor discourses on good and bad behavior. They need to develop a balanced organ for perceiving themselves and the world—"it is the aesthetic feeling that provides the seed out of which everything intellectual can grow."[212]

All this develops through the teacher's example ("Children experience the world *through the teacher*, the world in its goodness and in its wickedness, in its beauty and in its ugliness, in its truthfulness and its untruthfulness."[213]) and is conveyed directly to the child's rhythmic system:

People who learned as children to feel sympathy for what is good and antipathy for what is evil, who learned to feel enthusiastic about what is good and repulsion for what is evil, will have absorbed into their entire rhythmic organism a sense of what is good and what is bad. They will later feel that they cannot breathe when there is evil, that it takes their breath away and that their rhythmic system suffers.[214]

Rudolf Steiner pointed out that as teachers we can and should not only be the "gateway to the world" and "represent the world," to the children, but also represent to them the "goodness, truth, and beauty" in the world. "[...] You cannot educate and teach children of that age if you are not the accepted authority, if the children do not feel that everything that you think is true, is true; that what you find beautiful must be beautiful; and that things are good because you consider them to be good. You must represent the good, the true, and the beautiful to the children. Children must be drawn to goodness, truth, and beauty because they are drawn to you."[215] In what we are, in our morality, we are examples to the children; and in our teaching we can develop images of a "good, true and beautiful" life that conveys inner moral standards. In a lecture about the moral development of children and the importance of teaching that Rudolf Steiner gave in Oxford on August 19, 1922, he said:

> We must not force moral judgments on children; we merely lay the foundation so that when children awaken in puberty they can form their own moral judgments by observing life. The least effective way to attain this is by giving children finite commands. Rather, we work through examples or by presenting images to their imagination—say, through biographies or descriptions of good or bad people; or by inventing circumstances that present a picture of goodness to their mind. Because the rhythmic system is especially active in children during this period, pleasure and

displeasure can arise in them, but not judgment of good and evil. They can experience sympathy with what is good in an image, or a feeling of antipathy toward the evil in an image. It is not a matter of appealing to children's intellect by saying, "Thou shalt..." or "Though shalt not...." It is rather a matter of nurturing aesthetic judgment, so that children begin to feel pleasure and sympathy when they see goodness and feel dislike and antipathy when they see evil.[216]

*

Rudolf Steiner described the "love for the teacher," the relationship that is based on sympathy, as the fundamental condition and "vehicle" for the internalization of individual learning contents and objectives.[217] In his meetings with teachers and students he strongly urged them to foster that particular quality of the pedagogical relationship in the course of the second seven-year period and to ensure that it survived the crisis ("...we must make every effort inwardly to achieve with our art of education that children continue to see our authority as justified between the change of teeth and puberty."[218]).

The pedagogical relationship needed in the second seven-year period, and in puberty (its transformed equivalent) and adolescence,[219] is not there from the start. It has to be built up in the first school years when the transition takes place from the principle of imitation that governed the preceding developmental stage to the stage when the children orient themselves toward the personality and essence of the teacher and to the teacher's words, which shape the lessons and which they take in with growing *consciousness*: "When children enter school, something of the former physical-religious mood is still at work [...], something of their longing to take in everything that is going on around them. This perception, which elicits imitation, now merges with the intense listening to what the teacher as the pedagogical authority brings to the child."[220] Rudolf Steiner described this process as the "transformation of instinctive imitation into the capacity of appropriation on the basis of a natural relationship to authority."[221] Children, as he pointed out, tend toward a "sense of authority" after the change of teeth but still retain their "desire" to imitate for some time. ("... so that the children's urge to imitate their surroundings is continuously intermingled with their urge to let an authority work on them."[222]) According to Rudolf Steiner, this transition, or necessary penetration of the principle of imitation by the principle of authority,[223] takes place during the first two (to three) school years, up to the child's ninth year.[224] — "...when children enter school we observe, up to the age of nine—approximately—how children still feel the urge to imitate, while feelings of devotion for an authority are emerging powerfully. If we are able to observe how these two fundamental forces interact in the growing child we will learn from life what we need to teach and how we need to teach it."[225] Rudolf Steiner described also how essential an *artistic* teaching approach was for this "interaction of the two fundamental forces" and the successful transition to accepting the teacher on the basis of authority:

> We will be best able to do justice to this interaction of the principles of imitation and authority if we cultivate an artistic approach to teaching, because an artistic approach has elements of imitation as well as elements of human interaction. If we want our teaching to be artistic it has to pass from individual to individual. We stand differently in front of the children if everything we want to bring to them is pervaded by an artistic element. By teaching in this way we bring something of our own substance into the lesson that the children perceive as authority. This means that we are not just copying a conventional culture but that we meet the children person to person, and then they will naturally accept our authority.[226]

Teachers who transform what they teach into artistic images by drawing pictures on the blackboard and relating contents freely in a convincing and *creative* way will meet the children person to person, as individualities. Those teachers do not teach abstract "objects" of the world with passive detachment, but have—actively and creatively—developed what they bring to the children, and take responsibility for it. From such a living process, the teacher arises as a "natural authority." And so, there is no need to establish who is in charge and to implement sanctions.

*

By the time the children, in their ninth or tenth year, experience the radical change in their perception of themselves and the world that is accompanied by the inner crisis, the pedagogical relationship with their teacher has been firmly established. Rudolf Steiner pointed out repeatedly that this relationship is necessary and that the children expect it. In Waldorf schools the *continuity* in the teaching relationship at this stage is seen as crucial, while in other systems the children change to "secondary schools" at just this time. Steiner saw it as important that class teachers remain with their children for eight years, until they reach "earth maturity."[227]

During the crisis that occurs around the ninth year children often turn to the teacher in a subtle way because they go through a period where they feel an inner insecurity:

> Children of this age often come to their beloved teacher with some kind of a problem. They often don't even speak of their worries, but of something totally different. We need to know that there is something that troubles the child deep inside and we have to find the right answer, the right attitude. The way we respond can affect the child's whole life.[228]

In these situations it is not so important what the children ask. The children are not usually able to put into words what really troubles them because they are not consciously aware of what it is. It is more important to give them attention: "What the children ask is often of little significance. It is the fact that they ask, that they come to us in this way, that is very significant indeed...."[229] In various lectures that he gave to teachers, Rudolf Steiner described this situation, which we need to recognize and in which we need to find the right words and the right pedagogical response. Even if the children, as often happens, do not turn to us at all, it is still one of our most important tasks to be aware of their situation and to respond in a subtle way. When we "answer" the question, whether it has been asked or not, it is again not the content of our response that counts but the relationship and the attitude that comes to expression through it:

> The children grow insecure, and as teachers we have to respond to this through our attitude. We do not even have to think of something special to do, we only need to do what we do with special love, or address the child with special consideration at this particular moment, so that the child feels: the teacher loves me. We recognize the child's situation at this age, and in doing so we help him or her to overcome an obstacle.[230]

Rudolf Steiner often emphasized the importance of this meeting, a meeting that might seem insignificant but that has a deep impact on the child's later life: "The child's whole later life depends on what we [as teachers] do in this moment of crisis—whether the children will later be enthusiastic and confident about life, or remain detached and inwardly rigid."[231] "It is of great importance for the child's later life that the teacher finds the right attitude to the child who is between the ninth and tenth year."[232]

Without wanting to appear fatalistic, Rudolf Steiner tried to explain how much a genuinely felt reassurance from the revered teacher (who represents the "gateway to the world") means to children who go through this experience of insecurity. If this reassurance was not successful, the insecurity of this "moment of crisis" might persist through life. As Steiner warned: "[...] whether a child grows to be weak or stand firmly in life sometimes depends on whether the teacher finds a sufficiently safe way of responding to the child at that point in time."[233] The experience of insecurity in the middle of childhood, when the children long for the support of another person, can therefore have a lasting effect—at a deeper, hidden level—on their character, temperament and physical health: "Whether people can be enthusiastic in crucial situations or whether they carry an inner emptiness through their lives depends in many—not all— respects on how their teacher or educator behaved toward them around their ninth or tenth year."[234]

Steiner repeated in this context that it was not necessary for teachers to have profound conversations with the child in question or to make dramatic interventions. It is more a matter of developing a special "inner sensitivity" for the particular situation of the child and for how one should respond to it: "It is a matter of simply finding the right word at the right time, when we meet, say, in the corridor a boy or girl who asks a question—that we look at them in the right way when we answer. The art of education—just like painting, sculpting, or any other art—cannot be learned or taught in an abstract way. It is founded on an infinite number of details that arise out of an inner sensitivity. We can develop this inner sensitivity if we practice anthroposophical spiritual science."[235] We can gain inner sensitivity from anthroposophy because anthroposophy offers us a key to the being of the child, to child development and the needs of children; in this case, to the situation around the ninth or tenth year that we can learn to understand, even physiologically, if we develop the right faculties and awareness in us. Rudolf Steiner did certainly not imply that Waldorf teachers or anthroposophists automatically possess the sensitivity and tact that is needed to find the "right word" and the "right way of looking at the child" at the "right time." But he knew that the true study of the human being combined with a profound relationship with the child and love for the child are necessary preconditions for the ability to understand where the children are and to act out of this understanding—through the artistic presence of mind that should be the hallmark of every Waldorf teacher.

*

When Rudolf Steiner described the crisis of the ninth to tenth year and the pedagogical challenges that it involves, he pointed out that children not only depend on the personality of the teacher at that stage, they also begin to question it. The child's feeling of insecurity, which arises from the dramatic changes in how the world and the child's own self are experienced and from the process of establishing an inner rhythmic balance, extends also to the teacher and to the pedagogical relationship. That relationship is an integral part of the general instability and is no longer naturally accepted. Steiner said that the child experienced a "crisis of the authoritarian principle" at this age.[236] The children's trust in authority that grew out of the imitation principle of the first school years is somewhat shaken and undergoes a natural crisis due to the child's situation.[237] If children are unable to maintain or re-establish the relationship with the teacher it will have consequences for the lessons and for their general development, especially in the moral realm. Steiner spoke of a potential "instability" in the child's moral character as a result.[238]

Steiner elaborated on the "crisis of the authoritarian principle" that children experience in the middle of childhood. It differs essentially from the rebellion of adolescents:

[During the first years of school] the children's relationship with authority is undifferentiated. They accept authority and feel the need to subject themselves to it. Once they have reached the age of nine something special happens, and the children now want to see the authority justified in some way. Do not misunderstand my meaning. Children would not intellectually consider whether an authority is justified or not. Something emerges in the child's feeling life that makes it necessary for the authority to prove itself, to prove that it is properly founded in life and that it is sure of itself.[239]

Up to that point the children did not notice whether we are clumsy teachers, whether we tend to walk into things or drop the chalk, and so on. They would not think about a habit such as one preacher developed who kept on touching his nose after each sentence, which made him look ridiculous to the congregation. Although some children notice these things before they turn nine, they do not leave a deep impression. It would, however, be wrong to think that they remain unnoticed. When the children have reached the age of nine, they begin to be acutely aware of such things.

Later, when the children are ten or eleven, they return to paying less attention to such things. But now, at this point in life, they are acutely aware of such habits and they include them into the whole array of questions that begin to trouble their souls at this age. The questions might never be voiced but they are there nonetheless. The children wonder inwardly whether we are competent, whether we are firmly grounded in life and whether we know what we want. They are highly sensitive to our whole personality.

We will have a totally different effect on children depending on whether we are skeptics or true believers. If we are skeptics something different will speak out of our voice. Children are concerned with such things between the ninth and tenth year. The individuality begins to gain importance. A teacher with an orthodox protestant outlook will make a different impression from a catholic teacher, because their souls are tuned in different ways.[240]

The children begin to "test" our qualities as teachers, our habits, our presence, and our "general soul situation." Before, we were for the children, if they had developed rightly and in an unspoiled way, a "gateway to the world," mediators and representatives of the world. This role is now for the first time called into question. The children lose their former certainty and grow doubtful and skeptical. Our previously unquestioned position of authority begins to sway: "The children really begin to have doubts about us, even though they are unconscious doubts. They want to know whether we really carry the world within us, whether we have—so far—been worthy representatives of the entire cosmos."[241]

*

As with all the changes and processes of this developmental stage, the "testing" of the teacher that Steiner described is not a cognitive event but takes place in the child's semi-conscious realm of feeling. It goes far beyond the aspects described earlier. The foundations of our teaching, the basis and background of our knowledge are called into question. Rudolf Steiner wrote in his notebook:[242] "Age 9: from the person of the teacher to the source of teaching." In lectures he explained:

Now, between the ninth and tenth year, children feel instinctively in their subconscious: I receive everything from the teacher. Where does the teacher get it from? What stands behind the teacher?[243]

These are not conscious thoughts, they are vague feelings. Children cannot put them into words, but they are there nonetheless. What is it that speaks unconsciously out of the children? Before, they felt: things are good or bad, right or wrong if the teacher says they are good or bad, right or wrong. They are beautiful or ugly depending on whether the teacher likes them or not.—The teacher naturally sets the standard. At this point in time, between the ninth and the tenth year, this inner certainty is shaken. A question appears in the child's soul: Where does he or she get it from? What about the teacher's authority? From where is this authority?[244]

"I perceive the cosmos through this authority. Is the authority justified?" Children feel this question inwardly over weeks and months.[245] "Their belief in the good teacher" begins to falter.[246] Their doubts, though they do not rise to the surface, relate to the teacher's position, ideological foundations, and spiritual background: "The teacher begins, if I may use this image, to become transparent. The child wants to see the world that lives behind the teacher,"[247] Steiner said; and added that children tested "unconsciously" whether the teacher was able to "represent" the world. From now, if the education is to proceed in the right direction, the children must not only be able to accept, but also to recognize the teacher's position. Children expect teachers "to prove their authority to a perception that has grown more mature."[248] The authority that they previously followed naturally is individualized now. After their successful passage through this biographical strait, they need to be able to trust and love this authority,[249] because out of this newly consolidated trust their soul life will find new stability. For this to happen, the crisis needs to be weathered and the pedagogical relationship must be newly established:

What the children's inner being asks of us is that they can believe in us, that they can have the inner certainty: this person who stands next to me and tells me things, can tell me these things because of his relationship to the world. He is the mediator between myself and the entire cosmos. [...]

For the children, the teacher is the mediator between the divine world and their own powerlessness.[250]

Steiner once said: "Children feel an inner urge at this moment to break through the visible outer person, who was a god for them until now, to the supersensible or invisible god or divine being that stands behind the teacher."[251]

*

As teachers, we need to regain the child's recognition or trust that has now become more conscious and "mature." Again, this is a process that often happens in a hidden way. It is certainly not the task of Waldorf teachers to justify their authority, or rather, the sources of their authority: "It can be harmful if teachers begin to offer definitions and explanations. It is more important that we find for the child a warm, soul-imbued word—or words, since the difficulties usually persist for some weeks or months—so that we can maintain our authority while the children overcome this obstacle. It is a crisis of the authority principle for the child. If we prove equal to this challenge and know how to meet the difficulties that appear at this moment in life with the right amount of inwardness, credibility, and authenticity, we will be able to maintain our authority. This is valuable because the children can continue to trust in our authority, which, again, is advantageous for our further teaching; but, more important, because it is essential that the children at this age do not lose their belief in the goodness of humanity, as otherwise the inner trust that they will need in life will be shaken. These are immensely important considerations and we need to take heed of them. Knowing what happens at this time and how to respond to it in the right way so that the beacon of our behavior can shine through the child's future life is much more important than knowing all the finicky details that we read in pedagogical textbooks."252

When Steiner said that it is a matter of meeting the child "with the necessary inwardness, credibility, and authenticity," he did not mean that we should simply try to be "natural" and "human," but that we make a real effort to work out of our highest ideals and spirituality. We not only have to meet the children with the "right feeling of soul," but we have to *prove* ourselves. We need to be able to reveal the profound essence of what we have taught since the beginning of school. For the children it is important that there is an inner connection between the teacher and the lesson content. There has to be a congruence between the word and the individuality. The knowledge about the world that has been taught for some years becomes questionable because the teachers themselves, their authenticity, and spiritual capacity, become questionable for the children who have grown insecure and lost their natural acceptance of the world and everything in it. On July 22, 1924, Rudolf Steiner said in a lecture on education in Arnhem, Holland: "We must meet the children now in a way that gives them the feeling that something higher is standing behind us, that we are not just saying arbitrary things, but that we are messengers of the divine. The children must be able to feel this, and they will feel it least of all if we simply lecture to them. It is more effective if we speak in a particular tone of voice, even if we say something less important, so that the children realize that we have a heart and that in our heart we believe in what stands behind us. Then we will achieve something. The children must really feel that we are standing firmly in the world. Children will ask questions at this age, and they will understand something, even if they are not yet able to take in abstract, rational ideas. We can speak to them about how we receive from the sun what we give them, that without the sun we would be unable to give them anything; that we would not be able to give them anything without the moon, too, which preserves in a divine way in our sleep everything the sun gives us. While we might not say anything important in terms of intellectual content, if we say it warmly so that the children realize that we love the sun and the moon, we will have answered their question in a way that will be an inspiration for their further life."[253]

Rudolf Steiner also emphasized that we have to grow as teachers during this time. He said that "through our new attitude" we should convey to the children the feeling and conviction: "The teacher knows even more than I thought!" Steiner expected of Waldorf teachers not only to become aware of and lovingly accompany the child through the crisis of the ninth or tenth year, but demanded that they actually grow beyond themselves and to widen their knowledge and skills to an extent that would surprise the children. This is not about demonstrating results and achievements, but about breaking through what has lived in the personal relationship so far, about overcoming stale routines that might have found their way into the teaching routine. If as teachers we approach the crisis at this age consciously, we will be able to make good pedagogical use of this time and give the children something essential that will surprise them and confirm their affection for the teacher:

> If the children know that we as teachers can grow, that we have not yet shown them all we can do and given them all we can give—we might say something confidentially to surprise a child, so that the child becomes interested and listens to what is new in what we have said—we will have achieved the right relationship. We need to hold something in store that will surprise the children at this particular time and that will allow us to grow in the eyes of the children. It is the answer to one of life's essential riddles that we are able to grow beyond ourselves at this time. It is a comfort to children and gives them strength because they expect it of their teacher, whom they have grown to love.

Other teachers will have the bitter experience that their authority dwindles away into thin air when the children reach the ninth and tenth year.[254]

*

In his pedagogical and anthroposophical writings and lectures about the middle of childhood, Rudolf Steiner indicated occasionally that relationships other than with their teachers can be important at this time: "It is important that the children find somebody—one person or several—who continues to live in their memory as an example for their future life."[255] There were various people like that in Steiner's life, for example the assistant teacher in Neudörfl who introduced him to music and artistic drawing and who gave him a geometry book that introduced essential aspects into his life at this developmental stage. (The teacher could also be found in the teachers' room and was available for personal conversations). And there was a physician from Wiener Neustadt who came to see patients in Neudörfl. He opened up a new world to the inquisitive young son of the station master by telling him about German literature and aesthetics while he was waiting for his train home:

> He liked to talk to me; often, after he had rested a while under the linden trees, he would take me aside and we would pace back and forth near the station while he talked about German literature—not pedantically but full of enthusiasm. In those discussions he developed all kinds of ideas concerning the beautiful and the ugly.

> Another memory I have always deeply cherished is of the tall, slender doctor with the vigorous step, who always carried an umbrella in his right hand so that it dangled next to his body at one side, while on his other side I, a boy of ten, was completely absorbed in what he was saying.[256]

These encounters with people to whom one relates in the middle of childhood have an essential value for the entire biography. They help give stability to children in a crisis situation and consolidate their relationship with their own self *and* with the world. Re-emerging as memories in later life, these memories are woven into our biographies as events, they give substance to our life and provide continuity in our destiny. As Rudolf Steiner points out:

Few people notice what I am about to describe, but it occurs again and again that at certain times of life childhood impressions rise to the surface. Images from this turning point in life between the ninth or tenth year are particularly significant, whether they appear in later life in our dreams or when we are awake, whether they are vague or clear, whether we look at them with sympathy or antipathy. It is not the sympathy or antipathy as such that is important but the fact that there is something in the child's soul that turns into sympathy in one instance and into antipathy in another. It is not even necessarily the entire process, the entire memory from this turning point in life that is explicitly conscious; in fact, it is often wholly unconscious. But the process does take place. Those who tend to have vivid dreams will have recurrent dreams of a scene or of a personality, a guiding individual who once came as a helper into our life when we were children and guided or warned us, awakened trust in us, and with whom we established a personal relationship.

Children need such encounters between the ninth and tenth year because of the objective transformation they experience at that time. Up to that point they were one with the world around them, now they feel the need to have their own soul life, to be an individual who meets the outside world.[257]

Those who have true insight in human nature and are able to observe the etheric time organism throughout a whole human life, as I have described it, will know that when people grow old and become contemplative, they look back over their lives and see how pictures rise up from among the images from early childhood of people who had a particular influence between the ninth and tenth year.[258]

*

Notes

Translator's note: references to the works of Rudolf Steiner refer to the pages of the German edition (GA). Quoted passages have mostly been newly translated or, if taken from earlier translations, adapted in style and terminology. For a list of English titles see the Bibliography.

1   Quoted from Hans Müller-Wiedemann: *Mitte der Kindheit. Das neunte bis zwölfte Lebensjahr. Beiträge zu einer anthroposophischen Entwicklungspsychologie.* Stuttgart 1989, p. 74f.

2   GA 301, p. 124.

3   GA 310, p. 73.

4   GA 304, p. 161.

5   GA 311, p. 41.

6   Cf. Peter Selg: *A Grand Metamorphosis. Contributions to the Spiritual-Scientific Anthropology and Education of Adolescents.* Tr. M. Saar and A. Meuss. Great Barrington MA 2008.

7   Cf. Hans Müller-Wiedemann's discussion of the deficient Fliessian "concept of latency" and of Erikson's psychoanalytical anthropological descriptions in: *Mitte der Kindheit. Das neunte bis zwölfte Lebensjahr. Beiträge zu einer anthroposophischen Entwicklungspsychologie.* Stuttgart 1989, p. 18ff. Müller-Wiedemann summarized: "Classical psychology, with its method of defining child development as a biological continuity in terms of gradually emerging intelligence structures, remained insensitive to the crises of childhood, as well as to the motifs and pedagogical needs arising from them. Behavioral psychology with its focus

on adaptation and conditioning has continued the process consistently." (Ibid., p. 37).

8   GA 304a, p. 45.

9   Cf. Peter Selg: *The Therapeutic Eye. How Rudolf Steiner Observed Children*. Tr. A. Meuss and M. Saar. Great Barrington MA 2008.

10   GA 310, p. 107f.

11   GA 297, p. 264.

12   GA 302, p. 131.

13   Cf. Hans Müller-Wiedemann: *Mitte der Kindheit. Das neunte bis zwölfte Lebensjahr. Beiträge zu einer anthroposophischen Entwicklungspsychologie*. Stuttgart 1973.

14   Volume 1: *A Grand Metamorphosis. Contributions to the Spiritual-Scientific Anthropology and Education of Adolescents*. Tr. M. Saar and A. Meuss. Great Barrington MA 2008; volume 2: *The Therapeutic Eye. How Rudolf Steiner Observed Children*. Tr. A. Meuss and M. Saar. Great Barrington MA 2008; volume 3: *Willfried Immanuel Kunert. Zur Lebens- und Therapiegeschichte eines Kindes aus dem "Heilpädagogischen Kurs."* Dornach 2006.

15   GA 302, p. 134.

16   GA 294, p. 106.

17   GA 302, p. 131; emphasis added.

18   Ibid.

19   GA 24, p. 88.

20   GA 302, p. 132.

21   GA 294, p. 96.

22   GA 297a, p. 56.

23   GA 305, p. 21.

24   GA 304, p. 47.

25   GA 304a, p. 45.

26   Cf. GA 302, p. 133f.

27   GA 306, p. 89.

28   GA 301, p. 83.

29   GA 311, p. 37f.

30 GA 306, p. 109.

31 GA 302, p. 133.

32 Ibid., p. 134f.

33 For details concerning the balance of forces, cf. Peter Selg, "Der Wendepunkt des dritten Lebensjahres – Beiträge zur Genese des kindlichen Ich-Bewusstseins" in: Peter Selg, *Vom Logos menschlicher Physis. Die Entfaltung einer anthroposophischen Humanphysiologie im Werk Rudolf Steiners.* Dornach 2006, vol. 1, p. 352ff.

34 GA 311, p. 38.

35 GA 309, p. 74.

36 GA 307, p. 136.

37 GA 150, p. 17.

38 GA 294, p. 106.

39 GA 307, p. 202.

40 GA 302, p. 131.

41 GA 297a, p. 26.

42 GA 297, p. 172f.

43 Bruno Walter: *Thema und Variationen. Erinnerungen und Gedanken.* Quoted in Hermann Koepke: *Das neunte Lebensjahr.* Dornach 1997, p. 62f.; emphasis added.

44 Christy Brown: *My Left Foot.* London 1954, p. 53f.

45 GA 310, p. 67.

46 GA 304a, p. 45.

47 GA 294, p. 106.

48 Johnnie Quarrell. Quoted from Hans Müller-Wiedemann: *Mitte der Kindheit. Das neunte bis zwölfte Lebensjahr. Beiträge zu einer anthroposophischen Entwicklungspsychologie,* p. 73/287.

49 Pat Kirk. Ibid., p. 288.

50 GA 305, p. 19.

51 GA 307, p. 126.

52 GA 305, p. 19.

53 Jacob und Wilhelm Grimm: *Deutsches Wörterbuch.* Leipzig 1873. Vol. 5, column 2332.

54   GA 297, p. 179.

55   "Children who refer to themselves as 'I' for the first time, gain in this experience I-awareness within the spatial world of perception. It is remarkable that this experience, unlike that of the ninth year, is not remembered as *self-experience* but, as Jean Paul described, as light appearing in space: 'One morning, as I stood in the doorway as a very young child and looked to the left at the wood piled up there, a thought suddenly appeared before me like lightning from heaven that 'I am an I', and it has remained there as a shining light ever since. My I had *seen* itself for the first time and for ever.' [...] Around the third year the experience of one's own I seems to connect to the light of consciousness as 'from above.' Now the child says 'yes' to the earthly environment." (Hans Müller-Wiedemann: *Mitte der Kindheit. Das neunte bis zwölfte Lebensjahr. Beiträge zu einer anthroposophischen Entwicklungspsychologie*, p. 19). Elsewhere in his monograph Hans Müller-Wiedemann also quoted Jacques Lusseyran: "I see myself on my fourth birthday, as clearly as the picture that hangs before me on the wall. I was running on the pavement toward a triangle of light formed by the intersection of three roads, [...] toward the triangle of sunlight that opened onto Square Rapp like onto the sea. I was projected to this pond of light, absorbed by it, and while I still flailed my arms and legs about I said to myself: 'I am four years old, I am Jacques.' Call it the birth of the personality if you like. I did not feel any panic whatsoever while this happened. A ray of all-encompassing joy had hit me like lightning out of a blue, cloudless sky." (Ibid., p. 126).

56   For the concept of "biographical experience," cf. Hans Müller-Wiedemann in-depth study: "Was ist biographische Erfahrung?" in: *Mitte der Kindheit. Das neunte bis zwölfte Lebensjahr. Beiträge zu einer anthroposophischen Entwicklungspsychologie*, p. 28-37.

57 Karl Jaspers: *Schicksal und Wille*. Quoted from Hans Müller-Wiedemann, Ibid., p. 17. The German poet mentioned is Friedrich Rückert (1788-1866) and the original words of his poem are: "Aus der Jugendzeit, aus der Jugendzeit klingt ein Lied mir immerdar, ach wie liegt so weit, ach wie liegt so weit, was mein einst war."

58 Ernst Bloch: *Spuren*. Ibid., p. 22. Available in English as *Traces*, Stanford 2006, Tr. A. Nassar.

59 Oskar Kokoschka: *Mein Leben*. Quoted from Hermann Koepke: *Das neunte Lebensjahr*, p. 61f. Available in English as *Encountering the Self: Transformation and Destiny in the Ninth Year*. Great Barrington MA 1989, tr. J. Darrell.

60 Tony Hussey. Quoted from Hans Müller-Wiedemann: *Mitte der Kindheit. Das neunte bis zwölfte Lebensjahr. Beiträge zu einer anthroposophischen Entwicklungspsychologie*, p. 77, 289.

61 "We can express this in quite a radical way by saying: Children do not perceive other people whose movements, language, even feelings they used to imitate in an imponderable way before the change of teeth, as separate entities with their own inner essence. Up to the age of seven, children experience others as they do their own arms and legs. They do not see themselves as separate from the world. With the change of teeth, when the feeling life becomes independent through breathing and circulation, children separate themselves from others and others become individuals with a soul life of their own." (GA 303, p. 172f.).

62 Cf. GA 301, p. 207f.

63 Cf. chapter "Individuelle Reifung und Gruppenbildung" in: Hans Müller-Wiedemann: *Mitte der Kindheit. Das neunte bis zwölfte Lebensjahr. Beiträge zu einer anthroposophischen Entwicklungspsychologie*, p. 38-80 (in particular "Genius der Freundschaft," p. 38-47).

64 Ibid., p. 39.

65 Ibid., p. 40.

66   Hans Müller-Wiedemann pointed out that, already in the friendships of this lifetime, children experience aspects of the "duality" of their "identity," "of what I am and of what I can be, and what wants to manifest itself and grow in the everyday social intercourse with friends." (Ibid., p. 46).

67   Theodor Lidz: "The Person." Quoted from Hans Müller-Wiedemann: *Mitte der Kindheit. Das neunte bis zwölfte Lebensjahr. Beiträge zu einer anthroposophischen Entwicklungspsychologie*, p. 41.

68   Ibid., p. 46.

69   Ibid.

70   Ibid., p. 45.

71   Cf. Hermann Koepke: *Das neunte Lebensjahr*, p. 63ff. *Encountering the Self: Transformation and Destiny in the Ninth Year*. Great Barrington MA 1989, tr. J. Darrell.

72   Ibid., p. 60f.

73   For the biographical significance of these time rhythms, cf. Wilhelm Hoerner: *Zeit und Rhythmus. Die Ordnungsgesetze der Erde und des Menschen*. Stuttgart 1991 and Florian Roder: *Die Mondknoten im Lebenslauf*. Stuttgart 2005.

74   Self-report of a ten-year old Scottish boy, quoted from Hans Müller-Wiedemann: *Mitte der Kindheit. Das neunte bis zwölfte Lebensjahr. Beiträge zu einer anthroposophischen Entwicklungspsychologie*, p. 15.

75   Cf. Peter Selg: *Unbornness. Human Pre-existence and the Journey toward Birth*. Great Barrington MA 2010, tr. M. Saar.

76   GA 28. Rudolf Steiner, *Autobiography. Chapters in the Course of my Life 1861-1907*. Great Barrington MA 2006, p. 8, tr. Rita Stebbing (revised).

77   For Rudolf Steiner's important monastic relationships cf. Thomas Meyer: *Rudolf Steiners eigenste Mission. Ursprung und Aktualität der geisteswissenschaftlichen Karmaforschung*. Basel 2009, p. 17ff.

78   GA 28. Rudolf Steiner, *Autobiography. Chapters in the*

Course of my Life 1861-1907. Great Barrington MA 2006, p. 9, tr. Rita Stebbing (revised).

79 GA 303, p. 177.

80 Ibid., p. 178.

81 GA 317, p. 18.

82 GA 309, p. 41.

83 For the general physiological significance of the second dentition cf. Peter Selg: *Vom Logos menschlicher Physis. Die Entfaltung einer anthroposophischen Humanphysiologie im Werk Rudolf Steiners.* Vol. 2, p. 719ff.

84 For the physiology of the first seven years in general cf. ibid., p. 700ff.

85 GA 309, p. 59 and Peter Selg: *Vom Logos menschlicher Physis. Die Entfaltung einer anthroposophischen Humanphysiologie im Werk Rudolf Steiners.* Volume 2, p. 706ff.

86 GA 305, p. 21.

87 GA 309, p. 59.

88 GA 305, p. 20.

89 GA 317, p. 18.

90 GA 293, p. 168.

91 GA 302a, p. 56.

92 On the concept and general understanding of the "rhythmic system" in anthroposophical human physiology cf. Peter Selg: *Vom Logos menschlicher Physis. Die Entfaltung einer anthroposophischen Humanphysiologie im Werk Rudolf Steiners.* Vol. 2, p. 604ff.

93 GA 210, p. 233.

94 Cf. Peter Selg: *Vom Logos menschlicher Physis. Die Entfaltung einer anthroposophischen Humanphysiologie im Werk Rudolf Steiners.* Vol. 2, p. 700ff.

95 GA 303, *Soul Economy and Waldorf Education.* Tr. R. Everett, adapted by M. Saar. Great Barrington, MA 2003, p. 141f.

96 GA 307, p. 157f.

97 GA 293, p. 175.

98   GA 311, p. 116.

99   In: *Beiträge zur Rudolf Steiner Gesamtausgabe* No. 21, p.
      8.

100   Cf. Peter Selg: V*om Logos menschlicher Physis. Die
      Entfaltung einer anthroposophischen Humanphysiologie
      im Werk Rudolf Steiners.* Vol. 2, p. 604ff.

101   GA 311, p. 63/110.

102   GA 306, p. 110.

103   Ibid., p. 63.

104   GA 308, p. 49. Although Rudolf Steiner did not elabo-
      rate on this, it means that the heart organ plays a central
      part in the development of the child's rhythmic system,
      inner constitution and soul disposition in the crisis of the
      ninth to tenth year. Rudolf Steiner described the transfor-
      mation of the heart organ at that age in a lecture he gave
      in Dornach on May 26, 1922 (GA 212, p. 113ff). In the
      mediation between "upper" and "lower" organization
      it evolves increasingly as the organ of our "earthly con-
      sciousness" (GA 243, p. 57), cf. Peter Selg: *Vom Logos
      menschlicher Physis. Die Entfaltung einer anthroposo-
      phischen Humanphysiologie im Werk Rudolf Steiners.*
      Vol. 2, p. 625ff.), but also of our individual destiny with
      its interaction of feeling, memory and conscience (cf. Peter
      Selg: "Das Herzorgan und das Schicksal des Menschen.
      Zur geisteswissenschaftlichen Herzlehre Rudolf Steiners"
      in: Peter Selg: *Mysterium cordis. Aristoteles – Thomas von
      Aquin – Rudolf Steiner.* Dornach 2006, p. 105ff.). The
      crisis of the ninth to tenth year could also be defined as
      the time when the heart organ takes on its essential bio-
      graphical task. Children who master this crisis will be well
      equipped and able, once they have reached adolescence, to
      penetrate their ideas with soul forces and turn them into
      ideals that they are ready to put into practice. Cf. Peter
      Selg: *Der Wille zur Zukunft.* Arlesheim 2011, p. 43ff.—
      For the awakening consciousness of the heart organ in

children with heart conditions from the age of around ten see the remarkable clinical study of Herbert Plügge and R. Mappes: "Befinden und Verhalten herzkranker Kinder und Erwachsener," in: Herbert Plügge: *Befinden und Verhalten.* Stuttgart 1961.

105 GA 304a, p. 46.

106 GA 302a, p. 58f.

107 GA 317, p 18.

108 GA 206, p. 99.

109 In a lecture Rudolf Steiner gave in Dornach on August 7, 1921, he explained, among other things, that it is not until *after* the crisis of the ninth to tenth year that the higher members of the human organization are able to separate properly from the physical and etheric organism during sleep and that—with regard to life after death—the death of a child before this crisis is different from the death after this biographical change (GA 206, p. 102ff.).

110 Cf. note 104.

111 GA 306, p. 110.

112 GA 304a, p. 46.

113 GA 313, p. 70ff.

114 Ibid., p. 71.

115 GA 304, p. 198.

116 GA 305, p. 66.

117 GA 302a, p. 29f.

118 Ibid., p. 28.

119 Ibid., p. 29.

120 GA 306, p. 64.

121 GA 303, p. 161.

122 GA 304, p. 195.

123 For Rudolf Steiner's anthroposophical-physiological understanding of "soul body" or "astral body," cf. Peter Selg: *Vom Logos menschlicher Physis. Die Entfaltung einer anthroposophischen Humanphysiologie im Werk Rudolf Steiners.* Vol. 2, p. 478ff.

124 GA 303, p. 159f.

125 Ibid., p. 158.

126 Ibid., p. 176.

127 Ibid., p. 159; emphasis added.

128 Ibid., p. 158f.

129 GA 305, p. 109.

130 GA 303, p. 204.

131 Ibid.

132 Cf. Peter Selg: *A Grand Metamorphosis. Contributions to the Spiritual-Scientific Anthropology and Education of Adolescents.* Tr. M. Saar and A. Meuss. Great Barrington MA 2008.

133 For the physiological relationship of language to the rhythmic system cf. Peter Selg: *Vom Logos menschlicher Physis. Die Entfaltung einer anthroposophischen Humanphysiologie im Werk Rudolf Steiners.* Vol. 2, p. 610ff.

134 GA 310, p. 52.

135 GA 304a, p. 47.

136 GA 310, p. 52.

137 GA 304a, p. 41.

138 GA 310, p. 67.

139 GA 301, p. 144.

140 GA 304a, p. 126.

141 GA 309, p. 42. Cf. also GA 306, p. 62.

142 Cf. Peter Selg: *A Grand Metamorphosis. Contributions to the Spiritual-Scientific Anthropology and Education of Adolescents.* Tr. M. Saar and A. Meuss. Great Barrington MA 2008; and Peter Selg: *Der Wille zur Zukunft.* Arlesheim 2011.

143 GA 304a, p. 40.

144 GA 310, p. 142.

145 GA 314, p. 125.

146 GA 229, p. 75.

147 For the constitution of the second, "own" (as opposed

to inherited) body in the course of the second seven-year period cf. Rudolf Steiner's descriptions in: Rudolf Steiner: *Texte zur Medizin. Teil 1: Physiologische Menschenkunde.* (= Rudolf Steiner: *Quellentexte für die Wissenschaften.* Vol. 3). Ed. Peter Selg. Dornach 2004, p. 147ff. and 183ff.

148 GA 306, p. 156f.

149 Cf. Rudolf Steiner: *Texte zur Medizin. Teil 1: Physiologische Menschenkunde.* (= Rudolf Steiner: *Quellentexte für die Wissenschaften.* Vol. 3), p. 192ff.

150 GA 301, p. 86.

151 GA 297a, p. 26.

152 GA 304, p. 80.

153 Ibid., p. 152.

154 GA 306, p. 63.

155 Cf. Peter Selg: *Vom Logos menschlicher Physis. Die Entfaltung einer anthroposophischen Humanphysiologie im Werk Rudolf Steiners.* Vol. 2, p. 728ff.

156 "In everything that happens between teacher and child there must be a musical element; rhythm, beat, even the tune have to become a pedagogical principle. For this to happen teachers must have an inner musicality. It is the rhythmic system that predominates organically in children of school age. And our teaching must have a rhythmic orientation. We must have an inner musical orientation so that rhythm and beat can always prevail in the classroom. It must live within us instinctively." (GA 307, p. 122).

157 GA 305, p. 66.

158 GA 302a, p. 90.

159 GA 308, p. 40f.

160 Cf. also Eugen Kolisko: *Vom therapeutischen Charakter der Waldorfschule. Aufsätze und Vorträge.* Ed. Peter Selg. Dornach 2002.

161 GA 310, p. 81.

162 GA 303, p. 183.

163 Ibid.

164 GA 297, p. 48.

165 GA 310, p. 81.

166 GA 24, p. 88; emphasis added.

167 GA 310, p. 73.

168 GA 309, p. 71.

169 GA 303, p. 185.

170 GA 311, p. 46f.

171 GA 304a, p. 176 (Rudolf Steiner differentiated between "formative education" in the first seven years; "life-giving education" in the second; and "awakening education" in the third seven-year period. Ibid., p. 178).

172 GA 311, p. 49ff.

173 GA 304, p. 172.

174 GA 311, p. 56.

175 GA 294, p. 97.

176 Cf. GA 301, p. 192f.

177 According to Rudolf Steiner we cannot build on a true "Christian feeling" in religion lessons before the ninth year, or before the psychological and physiological crisis of the ninth/tenth year, as children only then begin to comprehend what stands behind the figure of Christ Jesus and are only then in a position to relate to the Mystery of Golgotha (GA 297a, p. 81). On August 15, 1923, Rudolf Steiner said in Ilkley, England: "If we want to give children a truly Christian upbringing we need to bear in mind that the Mystery of Golgotha and what it meant for the world, that the personality and divinity of Christ Jesus, cannot be presented to the child's soul in the right way before the child has reached the ninth or tenth year. We expose the children to great dangers if we do not introduce them before this moment in life to the general divine element in the world, to the divine father principle. We need to show the children how the divine lives everywhere: in nature, in the evolution of humanity, and in stones, but also in the hearts of people, in every deed that others do for the child. We must feel this

general divine principle ourselves with gratitude; and out of love and with our natural authority as teachers, introduce the children to it. Then we prepare the right approach to the mystery of Golgotha between the ninth and tenth year. [...] We prepare children in the best possible way to take in the glory of Christ Jesus from their ninth to tenth year, if we introduce them to the general divine element in the whole world before that" (GA 307, p. 207). Steiner said elsewhere (GA 297, p. 173) that this is the moment—when children become aware of their I in their ninth or tenth year—when the foundation is laid for their ability "to look up truly out of their innermost essence to the divine element that pervades the human soul and spirit." The ability to understand the Christ mystery coincides with the establishment of the rhythmic system (and the heart organism, cf. note 103). It was during his final illness that Rudolf Steiner wrote to a group of young physicians who had asked him about the relationship between the Christ being and respiration and circulation: "The heart blood that strives toward the breath in the lungs is the human being striving toward the cosmos. The breath in the lungs that strives toward the heart's blood is the blessing human beings receive from the cosmos. Blood that strives toward the heart is the refined process of dying. Blood that strives out of the human being as carbon dioxide, is the refined representation of dying. In this way the human being streams out into the cosmos continuously through the blood, a process that comes to radical expression after death when, out of the blood, it takes hold of the entire physical human being. [...] The Chr. mystery is the revelation of the great miracle that takes place *between* heart and lungs: The cosmos becomes a human being; the human being becomes cosmos. [...] What streams from the lungs to the heart is the human equivalent of Christ's descending onto earth; what brings strength from the heart to the lungs is the human equivalent of the Christ impulse that guides human beings into the spiritual world after death. We can therefore say that the Mystery of Golgotha lives in the human being organically between the heart and lungs." (In: Peter Selg: *Vom Logos menschlicher Physis. Die Entfaltung einer anthroposophischen Humanphysiologie im Werk Rudolf Steiners.* Vol. 2, p. 817ff. and Peter Selg: *Mysterium cordis. Aristoteles – Thomas von Aquin – Rudolf Steiner.* Dornach 2006, p. 129ff.).

178 GA 298, p. 134.
179 GA 310, p. 149f.
180 GA 296, p. 50.
181 GA 306, p. 110.
182 Cf. Peter Selg: *The Therapeutic Eye. How Rudolf Steiner Observed Children.* Tr. A. Meuss and M. Saar. Great Barrington MA 2008.
183 GA 298, p. 32.
184 GA 310, p. 37.
185 GA 305, p. 20.
186 GA 297a, p. 143.
187 GA 304, p. 104.
188 GA 302, p. 132; emphasis added.
189 GA 297a, p. 144.
190 GA 304a, p. 41.
191 GA 297, p. 165; cf. also GA 304, p. 105: "Children in their first seven years include their surroundings into all their activities by imitating primarily gestures, also inner gestures that are expressed through the spoken word. Children of school age, on the other hand, develop under the influence of what is conveyed to them through the word of naturally accepted authority."
192 GA 192, p. 191.
193 GA 301, p. 21; emphasis added.
194 GA 304, p. 105.
195 "You know that from the seventh year up to puberty, up to

the fourteenth, fifteenth year, children act under the influence of authority. It is most beneficial to children if they do what they do because people who they look up to say to them: it is right that this should be done. —Nothing is worse for children than being made to "decide for themselves" before puberty. The experience of being guided by authority between the seventh and fourteenth year must increase in the future. Education must strive with increased consciousness to awaken this pure and beautiful experience of authority in children. The seeds we plant in the children in these years will grow to be the foundation for a sense of equality in social life when they are adults. There will be no equality in the sphere of rights if the feeling of authority has not been implanted in them in childhood, because people will never be mature enough for such equality as adults. In the past, a lesser degree of authority might have been sufficient, but that will change in the future. We should instill the feeling of authority strongly into children so that they will grow to be mature enough for what is undoubtedly an historical requirement." (GA 296, p. 19).

196 Cf. Sergej O. Prokofieff: *Anthroposophie und "Die Philosophie der Freiheit."* Dornach 2006.

197 GA 304, p. 46.

198 GA 301, p. 203.

199 GA 297, p. 166; emphasis added.

200 "[...] *children need us, they need our humanity.*" (GA 305, p. 21).

201 GA 307, p. 135.

202 GA 304, p. 116.

203 Ibid., p. 162.

204 GA 304a, p. 102.

205 GA 311, p. 79 and GA 296, p. 22.

206 GA 304a, p. 42; emphasis added.

207 GA 302, p. 134.

208 Ibid., p. 129. Rudolf Steiner said about eurythmy in the

Waldorf school: "When children do eurythmy or when they sing, they continue the imitating activity of the earlier years while separating themselves from the imitation. They move. Singing and listening to music is in fact the kind of inner movement that also occurs in imitation. When we do eurythmy with children, instead of giving them only cognitive access when asking them to write the letters A or E down with pencil or pen, we enable them to write the content of words into the world with their whole body. We need to give children not abstract symbols, but to let them write into the world what they can write through their organism. In a sense, we enable them to continue the activity that they carried out before birth. By using images rather than abstract symbols when we teach children to read and write we do nothing that is alien to their inner being because we involve their inner being. By letting children move when they practice, we teach the whole human being." (Ibid.).

209 GA 304a, p. 140.
210 GA 308, p. 77.
211 GA 310, p. 54.
212 GA 305, p. 66.
213 GA 308, p. 78.
214 GA 307, p. 134.
215 GA 311, p. 41.
216 GA 305. Rudolf Steiner, *The Spiritual Ground of Education*, Tr. unknown, Great Barrington MA 1991. p. 52.
217 GA 306, p. 105.
218 GA 301, p. 83.
219 For the pedagogical situation in puberty and adolescence, cf. Peter Selg: *A Grand Metamorphosis. Contributions to the Spiritual-Scientific Anthropology and Education of Adolescents.* Tr. M. Saar and A. Meuss. Great Barrington MA 2008.
220 GA 306, p. 95.
221 GA 24, p. 86.

222 GA 297, p. 47.

223 GA 301, p. 82.

224 GA 297, p. 47.

225 Ibid., p. 166.

226 Ibid., p. 169.

227 This continuity, as Rudolf Steiner explained in England on August 15, 1924, allows teachers to return at a later time and in a more conceptual way to the contents that they had developed earlier artistically: "Nothing can be more useful and fruitful in teaching than giving children images in their seventh or eighth year and returning back to them in a different way once the children are in their thirteenth, fourteenth year. This is why we try in Waldorf schools to keep the children with the same teacher for as long as possible (GA 311, p. 63).

228 GA 311, p. 41.

229 GA 310, p. 107.

230 GA 307, p. 136f.

231 GA 84, p. 205.

232 GA 304, p. 79.

233 GA 303, p. 181. Hans Müller-Wiedemann, among others, pointed out that the inner instability that can result from failure to manage the crisis successfully (that is, when the crisis is not adequately perceived and accompanied by the adults in the environment) can manifest in different ways (also through increased adaptation to the—only remaining— "reality" of the external world). He wrote: "If this realm [of feeling] with all its insecurities, questions, and moral issues is not perceived by the educator, children will seek refuge in the cleverness that always gets through without being conspicuous, that adapts to behavioral patterns and learns to suppress experiences; or the experiences run along with the adapted behavior, unneeded and useless, causing melancholy and skepticism and the strange detachment that knows from early on that individual experiences do not count,

which easily turns into aggression and other psychological 'school illnesses' that will continue to reverberate through life." (Hans Müller-Wiedemann: *Mitte der Kindheit. Das neunte bis zwölfte Lebensjahr. Beiträge zu einer anthroposophischen Entwicklungspsychologie*, p. 32).

234 GA 297a, p. 56.

235 Ibid.

236 GA 311, p. 41.

237 GA 310, p. 108.

238 GA 304a, p. 46.

239 GA 304a, p. 46.

240 Ibid., p. 178f.

241 GA 306, p. 110.

242 GA 297a, p. 198.

243 GA 311, p. 41.

244 GA 310, p. 108.

245 GA 304a, p. 45.

246 GA 311, p. 42.

247 GA 306, p. 110.

248 GA 304a, p. 117.

249 GA 297a, p. 159f.

250 GA 305, p. 20.

251 GA 310, p. 108.

252 GA 311, p. 41f.

253 GA 310, p. 108f.

254 GA 306, p. 111f.

255 GA 303, p. 181; emphasis added.

256 GA 28. Rudolf Steiner, *Autobiography. Chapters in the Course of my Life 1861-1907*. Tr. Rita Stebbing (revised). Great Barrington MA 2006, p. 13.

257 GA 303, p. 181f.

258 GA 304, p. 153f.

Bibliography

Lectures or writings by Rudolf Steiner mentioned or quoted in this book, with English titles. All German originals are published by Rudolf Steiner Verlag, Dornach.

GA 24   *Aufsätze über die Dreigliederung des sozialen Organismus und zur Zeitlage 1915-1921* [Essays concerning the threefold division of the social organism and the period 1915-1921]: 2. Auflage 1982.

GA 150   *Die Welt des Geistes und ihr Hereinragen in das physische Dasein* [The world of the spirit and its extension into the physical world] (1913). 2. Auflage 1980.

GA 192   *Geisteswissenschaftliche Behandlung sozialer und pädagogischer Fragen* [Spiritual-scientific treatment of social and pedagogical questions] (1919): 2. Auflage 1991.

GA 206   *Man as a Being of Sense and Perception.* Tr. Dorothy Lenn. Vancouver, Canada: Steiner Book Centre 1981. In German: *Menschenwerden, Weltenseele und Weltengeist – Zweiter Teil: Der Mensch als geistiges Wesen im historischen Werdegang* (1921): 2. Auflage 1991.

GA 210   *Old and New Methods of Initiation.* Tr. J. Collis. London: Rudolf Steiner Press 1991. In German: *Alte und neue Einweihungsmethoden. Drama und Dichtung im Bewusstseins-Umschwung der Neuzeit* (1922): 2. Auflage 2001.

GA 212   *The Human Heart.* Tr. Not known. Spring Valley, NY: Mercury Press 1985. In German: *Menschliches Seelenleben und Geistesstreben im Zusammenhange mit Welt- und Erdentwickelung* (1922). 2. Auflage 1998.

GA 229   *The Four Seasons and the Archangels.* Tr. revised Pauline Wehrle. Forest Row, UK: Rudolf Steiner Press Fourth ed. 2008. In German: *Das Miterleben des Jahreslaufes in vier kosmischen Imaginationen* (1923): 8. Auflage 1999.

GA 243   *True and False Paths in Spiritual Investigation.* Tr. A.H. Parker. Hudson, NY: Anthroposophic Press 1985. In German: *Das Initiaten-Bewusstsein. Die wahren und die falschen Wege der geistigen Forschung* (1924): 6. Auflage 2004.

GA 293   *The Foundations of Human Experience* (previously: *Study of Man*). Tr. R. Lathe and N. Whittaker. Hudson NY 1996. In German: *Allgemeine Menschenkunde als Grundlage der Pädagogik* (1919). 9. Auflage 1992.

GA 294   *Practical Advice to Teachers.* Ed. tr. J. Collis. Great Barrington MA 2000. In German: *Erziehungskunst. Methodisch-Didaktisches II* (1919): 6. Auflage 1990.

GA 296   *Education as a Force for Social Change.* Tr. R. Lathe and N. Whittaker. Hudson NY 1997. In German: *Die Erziehungsfrage als soziale Frage. Die spirituellen, kulturgeschichtlichen und sozialen Hintergründe der Waldorfschul-Pädagogik* (1919). 4. Auflage 1991.

GA 297   *The Spirit of the Waldorf School.* Tr. Robert Lathe and Nancy Parsons Whittaker. Hudson, NY: Anthroposophic Press 1995. In German: *Idee und Praxis der Waldorfschule* (1919-1920): 1. Auflage 1998.

GA 297a   *Erziehung zum Leben.* [Education for life] *Selbsterziehung und pädagogische Praxis* (1921-1924): 1. Auflage 1998.

GA 298   *Rudolf Steiner in the Waldorf School.* Tr. Catherine E. Creeger. Hudson, NY: Anthroposophic Press 1996. In German: *Rudolf Steiner in der Waldorfschule* (1919-1924). 2. Auflage 1980.

GA 301   *The Renewal of Education.* Tr. Not known. Great
         Barrington, MA: Anthroposophic Press 2001. *Die*
         Erneuerung der pädagogisch-didaktischen Kunst
         durch Geisteswissenschaft (1920): 4. Auflage 1991.

GA 302   *Education for Adolescents.* Tr. C. Hoffmann. Hudson
         NY 1996. In German: *Menschenerkenntnis und*
         Unterrichtsgestaltung (1921):5. Auflage 1986.

GA 302a *Balance in Teaching.* Tr. R. Pusch and R. Querido.
         Great Barrington MA 2007. In German: *Erziehung*
         und Unterricht aus Menschenerkenntnis (1920-1923):
         4. Auflage 1993.

GA 303   *Soul Economy.* Tr. R. Everett. Great Barrington MA
         2003. In German: *Die gesunde Entwickelung des*
         Menschenwesens. Eine Einführung in die anthropos-
         ophische Pädagogik und Didaktik (1921/1922). 4.
         Auflage 1987.

GA 304   *Waldorf Education and Anthroposophy Vol. 1.* Tr. Not
         known. Hudson, NY: Anthroposophic Press 1995.
         In German: *Erziehungs- und Unterrichtsmethoden*
         auf anthroposophischer Grundlage. (1921/1922): 1.
         Auflage 1979.

GA 304a *Waldorf Education and Anthroposophy. Vol. 2.*
         Tr. Roland Everett. Hudson NY 1995. In German:
         Anthroposophische Menschenkunde und Pädagogik
         (1923/1924): 1. Auflage 1979.

GA 305   *The Spiritual Ground of Education.* Revised edi-
         tion. Great Barrington MA 2004. In German: *Die*
         geistig-seelischen Grundkräfte der Erziehungskunst.
         Spirituelle Werte in Erziehung und sozialem Leben
         (1922): 3. Auflage 1991.

GA 306   *The Child's Changing Consciousness and Waldorf*
         Education. Tr. R. Everett. Hudson NY 1988. In
         German: *Die pädagogische Praxis vom Gesichtspunkte*
         geisteswissenschaftlicher Menschenerkenntnis (1923):
         4. Auflage 1989.

GA 307   *A Modern Art of Education.* Tr. J. Darrell, G. Adams, R. Lathe and N. Whittaker. Revised edition. Great Barrington MA 2004. In German: *Gegenwärtiges Geistesleben und Erziehung* (1923). 5. Auflage 1986.

GA 308   *Essentials of Education.* Tr. not known. Revised by J. Darrell. Further revised by the publisher. Hudson NY 1997. In German: *Die Methodik des Lehrens und die Lebensbedingungen des Erziehens* (1924): 5. Auflage 1986.

GA 309   *The Task of the Teacher.* Tr. H. Fox, Ilkeston, n.d. In German: *Anthroposophische Pädagogik und ihre Voraussetzungen* (1924): 5. Auflage 1981.

GA 310   *Human Values in Education.* Tr. V. Compton-Burness. Great Barrington MA 2005. In German: *Der pädagogische Wert der Menschenerkenntnis und der Kulturwert der Pädagogik* (1924): 4. Auflage 1989.

GA 311   *The Kingdom of Childhood.* Tr. H. Fox. Revised by the publisher. Hudson NY 1995. In German: *Die Kunst des Erziehens aus dem Erfassen der Menschenwesenheit* (1924). 5. Auflage 1989.

GA 312   *Introducing Anthroposophical Medicine.* Tr. C. Creeger. Hudson NY 1999. In German: *Geisteswissenschaft und Medizin* (1920). 7. Auflage 1999.

GA 313   *Geisteswissenschaftliche Gesichtspunkte zur Therapie* [Spiritual-scientific viewpoints on therapy] (1921): 5. Auflage 2001.

GA 314   *Physiologisch-Therapeutisches auf Grundlage der Geisteswissenschaft. Zur Therapie und Hygiene* [Physiology and therapy based on spiritual science] (1920-1924): 4. Auflage 2010.

GA 317   *Education for Special Needs.* Tr. M. Adams. Revised. London 1998. In German: *Heilpädagogischer Kurs* (1924). 8. Auflage 1995.

Ita Wegman Institute
for Basic Research into Anthroposophy

PFEFFINGER WEG 1 A CH-4144 ARLESHEIM, SWITZERLAND
www.wegmaninstitut.ch
e-mail: sekretariat@wegmaninstitut.ch

The Ita Wegman Institute for Basic Research into Anthroposophy is a non-profit research and teaching organization. It undertakes basic research into the lifework of Dr. Rudolf Steiner (1861–1925) and the application of anthroposophy in specific areas of life, especially medicine, education, and curative education. Work carried out by the Institute is supported by a number of foundations and organizations and an international group of friends and supporters. The Director of the Institute is Prof. Dr. Peter Selg.